HOT HAND

Related Potomac Titles

Basketball on Paper: Rules and Tools for Performance Analysis by Dean Oliver

HOT HAND

THE STATISTICS BEHIND SPORTS' GREATEST STREAKS

ALAN REIFMAN

Potomac Books
Washington, D.C.

Library of Congress Cataloging-in-Publication Data
Reifman, Alan.
  Hot hand : the statistics behind sports' greatest streaks / Alan Reifman.
    p. cm.
  Includes bibliographical references and index.
  ISBN 978-1-59797-713-5 (hardcover; alk. paper)
  ISBN 978-1-59797-718-0 (electronic edition)
  1. Sports—Statistics. I. Title.
  GV741.R43 2011
  796—dc22

                                                           2011014068

Printed in the United States of America on acid-free paper that meets the
American National Standards Institute Z39-48 Standard.

Potomac Books
22841 Quicksilver Drive
Dulles, Virginia 20166

First Edition

10 9 8 7 6 5 4 3 2 1

To Sylvia, with love:

Being married to you is a perpetual winning streak.

CONTENTS

ACKNOWLEDGMENTS

Writing about the hot hand for roughly a dozen years—first in messages to online discussion groups, then on a blog, and now with this book—has been a true labor of love. Numerous people have supported me in this endeavor, many of whom I never would have met, but for my interest in the hot hand.

Tom Gilovich, a cofounder of "hot hand" research, has always been there to bounce off ideas and to fulfill requests (such as being the first guest of honor to field e-mailed questions from readers of my Hot Hand website for an online "chat"). *Curve Ball* coauthor Jim Albert (with his writing partner Jay Bennett) inspired me to conduct and write about sports statistical analyses, and also responded to questions from website visitors. Professor Jim Sherman of Indiana University, whom I first met in the spring of 1984 when I traveled around looking at graduate schools, later shared stories with me of how then–IU men's basketball coach Bob Knight reacted to the initial "hot hand" studies with skepticism, because so many factors go into shooting a basketball. Jim also invited me to a sports decision-making conference nearly twenty years after our first meeting, at which I met prolific "sabermetrics" baseball writers Bill James and Rob Neyer. Bill has never hesitated to share his streakiness-related analyses with me and let me post them on my blog, whereas Rob's mention of my analyses of the 2002 Oakland A's winning streak in one of his ESPN.com columns greatly increased my site's hit count. Two *Wall Street Journal* writers, Stefan Fatsis (during his NPR appearances) and "Numbers Guy" Carl Bialik, have also mentioned the site on multiple occasions. David Myers was one of the first academics to cite my "hot hand" analyses and has always written passionately on the topic. Phil Birnbaum's Sabermetric Research blog has been virtually a companion site to the Hot Hand blog, as we've referred each other to various sports-statistical studies over the years. I'm also thankful to members of the local Lubbock, Texas, media (Ryan Hyatt, Snead & Gus) who've had me on their radio shows to discuss the hot hand and various ongoing streaks. These, and other characters you'll meet in the book, have contributed their critical and analytic skills, and enthusiasm, to the study of the hot hand.

In the editorial arena, I thank Sylvia Niehuis, Michael O'Boyle, and Steve Reifman, all of whom read chapters of my original book manuscript and provided helpful feedback, and my editors at Potomac Books, Elizabeth Demers and Julie Gutin, and their associates. Last, I want to acknowledge friends and family members who have contributed in various ways over the years. My friend since childhood growing up in Los Angeles, Gregg Miller, still to this day lets me know whenever a UCLA team, athlete, or alumnus has some kind of streak going.

Finally, I would like to thank my closest family members for all their years of encouragement: my wife, Sylvia Niehuis; my parents, Estherly and Leonard Reifman; my sister Lynn (and her family) and brother Steve. My uncle Irv also offered some of his insights on horse racing, which have made it into the book.

I
Foundations

1

Introduction

The date was January 22, 2006. The Los Angeles Lakers were hosting the Toronto Raptors in a National Basketball Association (NBA) game. Lakers star Kobe Bryant had scored 26 points in the first half, a pace that would put him over 50 for the game, but the hometown fans were probably not in a jovial mood at that point. The Raptors, who came in with only 14 wins in 40 games, had led by 14 points at halftime and upped their advantage to 18 points a few minutes into the second half, 71–53.

With 8:41 remaining in the third quarter, Bryant hit a long two-pointer. At the 8:14 mark, Bryant lined up for a three-pointer. Good! At the 7:39 mark, he hit another shot from behind the arc, then another with 6:22 to go in the period! Next thing you know, Bryant had scored 27 points in the third quarter and the Lakers were now leading, 91–85. Ultimately, Bryant would add another 28 in the fourth, bringing his total to 81 points and propelling L.A. to a 122–104 victory.

Something special was going on in Oakland, California, in the latter part of the 2002 Major League Baseball (MLB) season. The Athletics, known as the A's, were on an amazing run, approaching an American League record 20th consecutive win. As Michael Lewis described the pregame scene on September 4 in his book, *Moneyball*:

> A traffic jam extraordinary even by Northern California standards stretched as far as the eye could see. The Oakland A's ticket office had never experienced anything quite like the crush of the previous two days. When the Kansas City Royals came to town, the A's sales department expected about ten thousand fans to turn up. In just the last twenty-four

hours more than twenty thousand people had stopped by, in the flesh, to buy seats in advance. Before the game, an aerial view of Oakland would reveal nearly everyone in sight heading toward the Coliseum.[1]

These two vignettes illustrate two things. First, streaks happen, sometimes reaching truly amazing lengths. Second, sports fans love streaks. (In this book, we will use both the everyday definition of "streak," as some result that keeps repeating itself several times in a row, and more formal statistical definitions that will be introduced later.)

Indeed, streaks are among the greatest accomplishments in sports. Allen St. John's 2006 book *Made to be Broken* reviewed 50 spectacular sports achievements (a year later, Michael Ferraro and John Veneziano released a similar book entitled *Numbelievable!*). St. John's list included Hank Aaron's overtaking of Babe Ruth's career home run record (later passed by Barry Bonds), and Bob Beamon's first-ever 29-foot-long jump in track and field (later passed by Mike Powell). Also presented were Wilt Chamberlain's 100-point NBA game in 1962 and Jerry Rice's National Football League (NFL) career record for touchdowns, both of which are still active records. A sizable subset (13) of the 50 legendary records cited by St. John, though, involve streaks, from Joe DiMaggio getting at least one hit in 56 straight games in 1941 to Coach John Wooden's University of California, Los Angeles (UCLA) basketball team winning 88 straight games in the early 1970s.

These kinds of achievements—along with miscellaneous other sports oddities—have been my motivation in maintaining the Hot Hand website on sports streakiness (http://thehothand.blogspot.com) since 2002. I also teach statistics at Texas Tech University, so I am able to blend my website with my academic interests. Over the years, I have been fortunate to have several media outlets do stories related to the Hot Hand website, including the *New York Times*, *Wall Street Journal* (online), National Public Radio (NPR), *Sports Illustrated on Campus*, the World Series program magazine, and even *Cigar Aficionado*. Now, having chronicled more than 350 streak-related stories on my blog, I would like to share some of them in this book.

SUSPENSE AND ENTERTAINMENT VALUE

One can enjoy streaks on many different levels, adding to the richness of the subject matter. For some sports fans, there's the suspense of whether a streak will keep going or end. Will he get a hit in the next game? Will she make her next shot? Will the team win (or lose) yet another game? Some streaks, of course, involve more pressure than others. If we're talking about a basketball shooting streak (such as Micheal Williams's NBA record of 97 consecutive made free throws)[2] or a baseball streak of hits in consecutive at-bats (the MLB record of 12, set by Mike "Pinky" Higgins in 1938 and Walt Dropo in 1952)[3], then the survival of the streak is at stake *each and every time* that person attempts a shot or comes to the plate.

Other streaks leave a little margin for error. With hitting streaks like Joe DiMaggio's, for example, as long as a batter gets multiple official at-bats in a game, he (or she, in the case of organized softball) can afford one or more outs during a game, as long as one hit is obtained. The suspense would only seem to reach fever pitch, therefore, when a player is up for what is likely his or her last at-bat in a game, having gone hitless thus far. Acknowledging that a consecutive-game hitting streak allows room for error should in no way diminish DiMaggio's accomplishment, of course. If it were so easy, someone else would surely have broken the record by now, but no one has. Why not?

Last, there are some streaks based purely on longevity, whose continuation doesn't depend at all on an athlete's performance in one specific opportunity (e.g., an at-bat in baseball or a shot in basketball) or even in a full game's worth of opportunities. In the 1990s, Cal Ripken Jr. of baseball's Baltimore Orioles not only broke New York Yankee Lou Gehrig's record of playing in 2,130 consecutive games, but Ripken extended the record to 2,632.[4] In this case, Ripken's accomplishment would appear to derive from at least three factors: (a) staying healthy for the roughly 16 years needed to compile the streak; (b) maintaining the quality of his play at a high enough level during this time period such that Oriole managers would have no inclination to bench him; and (c) determination to play every day, when other players might have asked for a day off. Though fans probably felt some degree of suspense as Ripken approached Gehrig's record—regarding whether Ripken could continue to avoid serious injury—I suspect that their fascination with Ripken's quest had to do with other factors. Fans presumably admired his work ethic and recognized that getting out of bed every morning to go to work is not always easy.

Readers may have noticed by now that many of the most famous streaks (or single nights of "hotness") have been compiled by athletes and teams who are among the all-time greats in their respective sports. In addition to Kobe Bryant, Joe DiMaggio, and the UCLA basketball program of 35–40 years ago, other major streak-holders include Tiger Woods (making the cut at 142 straight golf tournaments, over a period of 7 years) and the University of

Southern California (USC) and University of Miami football teams of the mid-2000s (each with 34 straight wins, the longest such streaks in roughly 30 years, with Oklahoma's 47 straight wins in the mid-1950s still standing as the all-time record).[5]

Although any long streak is likely to capture widespread attention, having a celebrated athlete or team involved almost certainly raises the entertainment value. The reason that legendary athletes and teams are often involved in major streaks is that they succeed on most occasions, simply by virtue of their over-whelmingly superior talent. Further, when the occasional bump in the road occurs, some kind of bizarre chance occurrence may give the athlete or team a lucky break that keeps the streak going. Many readers will recall the USC–Notre Dame football game of October 15, 2005, when the Trojans' 27-game winning streak appeared to be in jeopardy in the waning seconds, only to be saved by an unusual play in which a USC fumble rolled out of bounds, stopping the clock and giving the Trojans one last chance to win the game.[6] As the late Harvard paleontologist Stephen Jay Gould (about whom we'll hear more) once wrote, "Long streaks always are, and must be, a matter of extraordinary luck imposed upon great skill."[7]

STATISTICAL PERSPECTIVE

Another perspective for viewing streaks—my preferred one—is from a statistical or probabilistic view. When we observe some unusual occurrence, not just in the sports realm, but when, say, the same person wins the lottery twice, a common reaction is to ask, "What are the odds of that?" (We'll examine the lottery problem later, as it is analogous to how we can look at sports streaks.) Statistical analyses can be both simple and complex. Many of the formulas are pretty simple, such as that for the probability of rolling double sixes (or any particular matching pair) with a couple of dice. The probability in this case is simply 1/6 (the probability of a 6 on one die) multiplied by 1/6 (the probability of a 6 on the other die), which yields 1/36. This calculation can also be represented graphically, as a roll of 6-6 is one of 36 possible combinations of two dice (table 1.1).

However, probability analyses often involve a number of assumptions if they

Table 1.1

	1	2	3	4	5	6
1						
2						
3						
4						
5						
6						X

are to be applied in a given situation. For example, the dice-rolling illustration involves the assumption of *independence*, i.e., that the outcome of one die has no impact on that of the other die. One can therefore ask a seemingly straightforward question—*What was the probability of Joe DiMaggio going on a 56-game hitting streak, given his prior batting statistics?*—and find that different sports analysts arrive at different conclusions, depending on their assumptions. One of the upcoming chapters will focus on basic probability calculations, and another on the DiMaggio hitting streak.

To academic statisticians, probability calculations help answer another question: How likely is it that a given streak could have occurred by chance? After all, if one flipped a coin a thousand times, occasional "streaks" would occur, perhaps six straight heads or eight straight tails. To impress an academic statistician, therefore, one would have to show that a streak was so spectacular and so rare that it must be considered "beyond chance."

ORGANIZATIONAL CULTURE

Yet another lens through which to view streaks is that of organizational culture. The morning of Thursday, November 15, 2007, I was listening to the ESPN radio show *The Herd with Colin Cowherd.* The host was giving a commentary about how success stories such as pro football's New England Patriots (who would finish the regular season with a perfect 16-0 record) and disasters such as the Miami Dolphins (who would finish 1-15) don't happen by accident. Regarding the latter, years of poor drafting, a merry-go-round of coaches, and bad management decisions had taken their toll. Then on December 21, 2007, the Dolphins hired Bill Parcells, who had been a very successful coach with four different franchises.[8] While holding a high position in the team's front office, he essentially redesigned the team for the next season. Parcells hired a new general manager and coach, and brought about a major turnover in player personnel. The next season, the Dolphins went 11-5 and made the playoffs.

Cowherd's commentary reminded me of a book I had read about a year earlier, *Confidence: How Winning Streaks and Losing Streaks Begin and End*, by Harvard Business School professor Rosabeth Moss Kanter.[9] Kanter presented several case studies from corporate America and the sports world (including the Patriots), arguing that long-term success and failure—and turnarounds from one to the other—are heavily rooted in organizational culture. In the athletic realm, Kanter highlighted two women's collegiate teams, University of North Carolina soccer and University of Connecticut basketball, to present the most detailed case studies of winning cultures, as well as the Prairie View

A&M football squad to illustrate a losing culture. The Philadelphia Eagles' ascension in recent years to frequent Super Bowl contenders exemplified a turnaround. Kanter made several points about organizational culture, including the following:

- An organization's most visible results—on the scoreboard or in financial data—will tend to be reflected at a deeper level by other markers, such as a leader's communicative skills and ability to innovate (and spur innovation), and a team's work ethic, quality of facilities, community support, etc.

- Winning—or losing—can launch "chain reactions," thus perpetuating the original trend. Winning gets a team on television, helps attract better players (either through free agency in the pros or recruiting at the college level), builds fan support, etc., which fosters further winning, brings in money to improve facilities, etc. Losing sets the opposite types of events in motion.

- The ideal psychological environment for an organization seems to be one in which employees know they'll be held accountable for maintaining productive output, but feel supported enough that they will be comfortable taking risks, innovating, and reaching out to colleagues in a collaborative spirit. Failure of a promising idea to bear fruit will not trigger a cycle of criticism and blame, but rather a coming-together of employees to improve the next time.

While Kanter's ideas certainly ring true, the tricky part—which she readily acknowledges—is in untangling causation. Yes, a positive attitude (or nice facilities or fan support) can help a team win, but winning also promotes a positive attitude (and the ability to construct new facilities and to attract fans). Hence, we have a sort of chicken-and-egg problem.

ORGANIZATION OF THIS BOOK

Now that we're familiar with different ways of looking at sports streakiness, we can examine the topic in greater depth. Along the way, we'll look at some of the most famous and impressive sports streaks of all time. Our first stop on the rest of the journey, however, will involve a brief introduction to statistical methods used in analyzing sequences of sports performances to determine if the streaks they reveal are truly beyond what could reasonably come up just by chance. (If you're willing to accept the probability estimates I present throughout the book for various streaks, you can skip the statistics tutorial.)

Next, we'll consider evidence for a "hot hand," which we define as success by a player or team being followed by continued success (or failure being followed by failure, which would be a "cold hand") to an extent that cannot be accounted for by chance alone. In the chapters after that, we'll consider evidence against this concept. That streaks occur cannot be denied; it's just that there's a good deal of evidence that the streaks we see at sporting events don't run for any greater length than the streaks we see in simulated sequences such as coin flips. A series of chapters and mini-chapters will follow, providing case studies of extreme hotness and coldness, and of other sports oddities. Finally, we'll end by looking at two athletes whose names have come up so many times as I've worked on my Hot Hand website over the years that they must receive serious consideration as being among the streakiest performers in professional sports: baseball's Alex "A-Rod" Rodriguez and basketball's Kobe Bryant.

2

Statistical Methods

Throughout the book, I'll be providing estimates of the probability that a given streak could have occurred. Such calculations must take into account a couple of important factors. First, what is the previous track record of the player or team in question? For example, a long streak of consecutively made free throws by the smooth-shooting Ray Allen, a player who (at the time of this writing) has a near 90 percent career shooting percentage from the stripe, would be a lot less surprising than one by Shaquille O'Neal, the huge center who is dominant near the hoop but has hit only about 50 percent of his free throws over his career.

Second, any streak we observe on the court, rink, or field must be compared to what could have occurred purely by chance. Let's say, for example, that a professional women's basketball (WNBA) player makes seven straight three-point baskets in a game. We would start by looking over her career statistics (say she's been in the league for five years) and find, hypothetically, that she's consistently been a 40 percent shooter from behind the three-point arc. To emulate her career abilities, we could create an imaginary coin that comes up "hit" 40 percent of the time and "miss" 60 percent of the time. If she typically attempts 150 three-point shots in a season, we could flip our imaginary coin (probably via computer simulation) 150 times and see how often streaks of seven consecutive makes turn up. Only if her actual frequency of making seven straight three-pointers exceeds the frequency derived from the coin-flipping simulation could we say that she seems to be a streaky shooter.

In this chapter, we will go over various formulas and techniques for coming up with these kinds of statistical estimates. For the most part, they don't require any more advanced mathematics than basic arithmetic, taking percentages, and raising numbers to powers. For somewhat more advanced techniques, web-based calculators exist where the user can type in some numbers and receive a probability as the output. Again, however, if you just want to read about the streaks in the rest of the book without worrying about how the probabilities were obtained, you can skip this chapter.

COMPARING PERCENTAGES

Thanks to a 1985 article by Tom Gilovich, Robert Vallone, and Amos Tversky that introduced what we call "hot hand" research to the scientific community, one popular —and relatively simple—analytic technique is known as "p-hit-hit vs. p-hit-miss."[1] These stand, respectively, for probability of a hit (e.g., a made basket, or a hit in baseball) given a hit on the previous attempt, and probability of a hit given a miss on the previous attempt. These expressions are depicted formally as p(hit | hit) and p(hit | miss). If one defines a "hot hand" as a player experiencing a sustained rise in his or her success rate immediately following initial success (compared to his or her success rate following failure), then we should expect to find that p(hit | hit) exceeds p(hit | miss) when looking at the player's sequence (for a particular game or longer), attempt by attempt.

As an example, way back in 1998 I charted sequences of hits and misses in the NBA's All-Star Weekend three-point shooting contest. (Doing these kinds of recreational statistical analyses is what led to my creation of the Hot Hand website.) In the semifinal round, then Dallas Maverick Hubert Davis compiled the following sequence of hits (H) and misses (M), where the shots are grouped into sets of five attempts for ease of inspection, and shots that came immediately after a hit are underlined:

MH<u>HHH</u> <u>HH</u>MM<u>H</u> M<u>HHHH</u> <u>HHHHH</u> <u>HH</u>MM<u>H</u>

First, note that Davis made 19 of 25 shots overall (.76). Included were streaks of 6 consecutive hits and 11 consecutive hits. Any layperson, seeing 11 consecutively made shots, would say Davis had a "hot hand." Indeed, Davis's p(hit | hit) was an extremely high .83 (15 of 18). But because he had a high base rate for hits during the entire sequence, his p(hit | miss) was also high (.67; 4 of 6). The first shot does not contribute to either hit percentage, as it did not come after any other shot. The difference between .83 and .67 was not statistically significant (p = .38 according to a chi-square test, for those of you with some statistical training), so this sequence does not constitute a hot hand under Gilovich and colleagues' criterion. In order for p(hit | miss) to be low, of course, a player must exhibit long streaks of consecutive misses; this may be particularly hard to find among NBA-caliber players.

THE RUNS TEST

Another way to look at sequences of hits and misses is the runs test. Any un-interrupted sequence of hits or misses (e.g., hit-hit-hit or miss-miss-miss-miss) constitutes a "run." A sequence of hit-hit-*miss-miss-miss*-hit-hit-hit-hit would involve three runs, with each switchover from hit to miss initiating a new run. Streakiness would imply *few* runs in a sequence, as basketball shooters, baseball hitters, or other athletes considered to be "streaky" would be expected to string together bunches of successes during some parts of their performances, and bunches of failures during other parts. Some hypothetical sequences (each involving 10 hits and 5 misses) and their interpretations are as follows:

HHHHH MMMMM HHHHH (3 runs, more streaky)

HHMHH MHHMH HMHHM (10 runs, less streaky)

A statistical test determines whether an athlete's full sequence contains fewer runs than would be expected by chance, and hence whether there is evidence of streakiness. Professor Hossein Arsham maintains an online runs-test calculator, where the user can type numerical values (e.g., 1 = hit, 0 = miss) into an array of cells and receive immediate feedback as to whether the sequence of data represents streakiness or just randomness (http://home.ubalt.edu/ntsbarsh/Business-stat/otherapplets/Randomness.htm). Wayne Winston's book *Mathletics* provides a further tutorial on the runs test and other statistical approaches.

FORMULAS FOR ESTIMATION

A very simple concept is what I call the "perfect run." If a baseball player has five at-bats in a game and gets a hit every time (or goes hitless), that's a perfect run. If a football team plays 16 games and wins them all (or loses them all), that's also a perfect run. According to the textbook I use in teaching introductory statistics, "The probability of several particular events occurring successively or jointly is the product of their separate probabilities (provided that the generating events are independent)."[2] To make this more concrete, let's suppose a basketball player has a long track record, over the current season and previous ones, of making free throws 75 percent of the time (.75). That player's probability of making two straight attempts from the stripe is .75 × .75, which equals .56 (you'll notice this is also .75 squared). The probability of making three in a row would be .75 × .75 × .75 (or .75 cubed), which equals .42. As a more general rule, we are taking the probability (p) of success on each shot (in this case, .75) and raising it to a power equal to the length of the specific run (r), whether that be two, three, or some other number of shots. The probability of a perfect run is thus p^r. This formula *assumes independence of observations*, that the outcomes of any earlier shots have no effect on the probability of a later shot, just like the outcome of one tossed coin has no effect on the outcome of later tosses. Thus, even if our hypothetical free-throw shooter made seven in a row, this stretch of "hotness" would not raise the shooter's probability on the eighth shot above his or her usual success rate. That's why we can assign a constant probability of .75 to every shot. (Note that if we wanted to estimate the probability of this player *missing* three straight free throws, it would be $.25^3$, as the probability of a miss would be .25 for each shot.) We'll hear a lot more about the independence (or coin-tossing) model of sports performance; although it's controversial to compare human athletes to coins, an independence model has shown itself over a number of tests to produce results that provide a pretty good match to actual athletic performance.

When Each Attempt Has a Different Probability of Success: The Case of Different Golf Holes

When calculating the probability of a perfect run, the probabilities of success on each trial do not necessarily have to be the same. Unlike free-throw shooting, where the height of the basket and distance of the shot are constant, other sports such as golf present varying conditions. Take the example of Chad Campbell, who in the opening round of the 2009 Masters set a tournament record by getting a "birdie" (i.e., making the hole in one stroke less than par) on each of the first five holes. To provide context for what Campbell did, I estimated the chances of a typical Masters golfer breaking par on all of the first five holes. The number of golfers who broke par on each hole (usually by birdie, but occasionally by two strokes or "eagle") on the same day as Campbell was available online. Some holes seem to be easier than others for breaking par and, indeed, each of the five holes had a different probability of doing so. Seven golfers, out of ninety-six total, broke par on the first hole, yielding a probability of .07 (7 divided by 96). On the second hole, 46 golfers broke par, for a probability of .48, etc. Multiplying the probabilities for the five holes thus yielded the following calculation: .07 × .48 × .31 × .04 × .11 ≈ .00005 (approximately 5-in-100,000 or 1-in-20,000).

Simplicity is probably the main virtue of estimating the probability of a perfect run by taking p^r (as long as a suitable estimate for p is available). However, such an approach doesn't take into account the fact that, over the course of a full season, a player or team will generally have multiple opportunities to put together a streak of a given length. Giles Warrack, whose 1995 article "The Great Streak" represents one of the first statistical analyses of Joe DiMaggio's 56-game hitting streak, notes that the p^r term must be multiplied by the number of opportunities for starting a given streak.[3] Warrack states about the relevant equations: "The expression [for number of opportunities] represents the number of 'starts of streaks' for the player, the one when he starts his career, and then another . . . for each of the expected number of failures."[4] (For all you statistics instructors out there, Clifford M. Hurvich has created an online teaching handout based on Warrack's work.)[5]

Thus far, we have been concerned with the perfect run. Sometimes, though, an athlete or team can undeniably be hot or cold, but just a little short of a perfect run. The 2007 Colorado Rockies baseball team won 21 of 22 games spanning the latter part of the regular season and the playoff rounds leading up to the World Series (in which they were swept by the Boston Red Sox). UCLA center Bill Walton made 21 of 22 field-goal attempts in the 1973 National Collegiate Athletic Association (NCAA) championship game in leading the Bruin basketball program to another in its long line of national titles. (There's nothing magical about going 21 out of 22; both of my examples of near-perfect runs just happened to have these numbers!) Statisticians would frame this problem in terms of the probability of someone making 21 *or more* shots out of 22, given a prior baseline of success, as focusing on just one specific outcome (in this case 21 made shots) will almost certainly result in a very low probability. Let's simplify our look at near-perfect runs by asking what the probability is of a prior .60 shooter making at least three shots out of four. Here are the key steps:

1. The probability of a perfect run (making all four shots) is $.60^4 = .130$.
2. The probability of making three out of four, where .40 is the probability of a miss on any single shot is: $.60 \times .60 \times .60 \times .40$ (more formally, $.60^3 \times .40$), which yields .086.
3. We must take into account, however, that there are multiple ways to achieve a record of three hits (successful shots) and one miss. Namely, the miss could occur on the first attempt (MHHH), the second attempt (HMHH), the third attempt (HHMH), or the fourth attempt (HHHM). We would thus multiply the probability from the previous

step of a three hit–one miss sequence (regardless of the ordering of hits and misses), .086, by four, yielding .344.

4. We conclude by adding the probability of a three hit–one miss sequence (in all its possible orders) and the probability of hitting all four shots, which is .344 + .130, and that yields .474.

Readers who would prefer not to go through all the steps manually, especially for more involved examples than three (or more) out of four, can use the calculator at http://faculty.vassar.edu/lowry/binomialX.html.

REASONS FOR CAUTION

One must be very cautious in running straight for the calculator right after witnessing an unusual streak of wins, losses, hits, misses, or whatever. Think of the problem as one of sampling bias. We are not taking a random cross-section of games to see how often streaks occur, but rather seizing directly upon a presumably rare occurrence. Jim Albert and Jay Bennett's book *Curve Ball* gets right to the heart of the matter:

> The point we're trying to make is that we look at interesting baseball data and ignore noninteresting data, and that fact alone makes the interesting baseball data appear more significant than it really is. We say that inference from this [*sic*] data is biased, or misrepresentative of reality, since the data has been selected exactly because it appears unusual.[6]

One must also take into account the *opportunity* for something to have occurred. We may calculate that a particular streak had a 1-in-1,000 or 3-in-100,000 probability, for example. But when one considers that every year there are thousands of professional baseball and basketball games (just in the United States), never mind the countless individual pitches, at-bats, shots, etc., it is quite likely that certain streaks would be expected to occur every so often. This point is analogous to interpretations of the same person winning the lottery twice, as happened to a New Jersey woman named Evelyn Adams in 1985 and 1986. As textbook authors Bruce King and Edward Minium point out, the probability of a specific named individual such as Ms. Adams winning twice would be around 1 in 17 trillion;[7] however, research (by the statisticians Persi Diaconis and Frederick Mosteller) has shown that, with the huge number of people who play the lottery and number of drawings held, the likelihood of someone, somewhere, winning twice may be as relatively commonplace as 1 in 30.[8]

Having said all this, however, some streaks really do seem to go beyond what could be expected in the normal course of athletic competitions. After the Wake Forest men's basketball team made 50 straight free throws in January 2005, analyst Ken Pomeroy concluded the following:

> Assuming Wake Forest shoots 25 free throws a game, you would expect this event to happen to the Deacons once in every 66,000 games . . . 2,200 seasons . . . 110 generations.[9]

3

Evidence Supportive of a Hot Hand

So, what is the state of the evidence on whether athletes *really* can be streaky—in either a hot or cold sense—beyond what we would expect from a coin-flipping simulation? The importance of this question emerges from ESPN.com blogger Henry Abbott's hypothetical basketball coaching dilemma, involving whether to give the game-deciding shot in the closing seconds to a player who has a long-term shooting percentage of 40 percent, but who is 8 of 10 in the present game:

> If there is such a thing as "being hot," having nights when your muscles, form, and vision are freakishly in tune, then you have yourself an 80% shooter who needs the ball. But if there are just random short-term variations, then you could be entrusting the game to a low-skill player who has never been that good at shooting.[1]

Though it is unlikely that we could ever come up with a *definitive* answer to give our hypothetical coach, getting a handle on conditions that appear generally to be associated with streaky performance—or the lack of same—would probably be helpful. Accordingly, this chapter presents evidence for streaky athletic performance beyond chance, whereas later chapters present evidence against it. Indeed, there seem to be some clear differences between the situations in which true streakiness tends to occur, and ones in which it doesn't.

On April 12, 2009, as I was waiting for the television coverage of the Masters golf tournament to come on, I exercised my thumb by clicking the remote control to see what else was on. In doing so, I came upon a women's bowling event, just as one of the competitors, Carolyn Dorin-Ballard, was in the midst of a streak that ultimately stretched to 20 consecutive strikes.[2] The streak was said to be the longest ever recorded in a televised Professional Bowlers Association (PBA) event. Dorin-Ballard's streak, in and of itself, doesn't tell us that much about whether pro bowlers in general have a propensity to streakiness. Fortunately, however, rigorous, large-scale statistical research has addressed whether bowlers tend to be streaky (or, as I like to joke, whether they can get "on a roll").

The study in question, by Reid Dorsey-Palmateer and Gary Smith, appeared in a prominent professional journal, the *American Statistician*. Among other analyses, these authors examined data from the men's PBA competitions in 2002 and 2003 to see if bowlers had a higher probability of rolling a strike immediately following a series of strikes than following a series of non-strikes. Results showed that if a bowler had just thrown four straight strikes, his probability of striking on the fifth attempt was considerably higher (.612) than was his strike probability if his four previous attempts had all been non-strikes (.492). Taking the difference between these two percentages, one could say there was a "hot hand advantage" of .120 (or 12 percent). When a bowler had rolled three straight strikes (compared to three straight non-strikes), the hot hand advantage regarding the probability of a strike on the fourth attempt was 6 percent. The strike probability advantage on a third throw, based on throwing two straight strikes (compared to two non-strikes) was 3.6 percent. Finally, when a competitor was coming off a single strike (compared to a non-strike), he had a 1 percent greater probability of knocking all the pins down on the next ball, which over a large number of tournaments, could add up in the long run.[3]

Dorsey-Palmateer and Smith suggested that athletic skill tasks that are performed repeatedly at "regular, brief intervals" may be most conducive to hot hands.[4] Smith himself has studied horseshoe pitching and found success probabilities (i.e., tossing for a "ringer") to be inconsistent with an independence model.[5] Execution of other sports tasks that can be quickly and regularly repeated have also provided evidence supportive of a hot hand. In fact, David Gilden and Stephanie Gray Wilson made it a point in their laboratory to select operations with "minimal delay in the action [and in which] there is no interference."[6] One task they studied was golf putting, where they found some evidence of streakiness. Participants putted 300 balls from approximately 12 feet away in a self-paced fashion; the experimenter constantly fed balls back to the participant. When the putting records of hits and misses were analyzed statistically, 12.5 percent of the sequences exhibited significant streakiness, which is greater than the 2.3 percent that would be expected by chance. Gilden and Gray Wilson also studied dart throwing, but found it to be considerably less conducive to streakiness than golf putting. Part of the problem appeared to stem from the logistics of the procedures: "in the dart-throwing study, it was not possible for the experimenter to continuously supply the subjects with darts without incurring the danger of being hit."[7] Ouch!

Another type of athletic skill that lends itself to consistent execution over short delays is serving in tennis (granting that the combination of tossing the ball in the air with one hand and hitting the ball with the racquet in the other hand adds some complexity). Franc Klaassen and Jan Magnus, two economists from the Netherlands, examined point-by-point data from a number of men's and women's singles matches in the Wimbledon championships from 1992 to 1995 (encompassing a total of 86,298 points). They investigated whether there was evidence of streakiness in the server's likelihood of winning consecutive points, and indeed there was. As these authors summarized, "Winning the previous point has a positive effect on winning the current point for both men and women."[8] There are, of course, many ways for the server to win a point, ranging from an "ace" (a serve that travels so fast and is so well-placed that the receiver cannot even reach the ball), to balls returned so feebly that the server can quickly put the ball away to win the rally, to points won only after a long rally. I mention these possibilities merely to provide some background for my suggestion that players' potential ability to replicate powerful serves may account, in part, for Klaassen and Magnus's findings.

These findings make sense to me. Bowling, horseshoe pitching, and putting all involve brief, relatively simple arm motions—simple, at least, compared to more elaborate motions such as taking a full wind-up and throwing a pitch in baseball. When simple motions can be performed repeatedly in quick succession, these conditions presumably allow an athlete—once he or she has been successful on one attempt—to retain a motor memory of how his or her body executed the successful maneuver, and do it again and again. I performed a simplistic (probably overly simplistic) test of this idea in connection with the "hardest shot" contest at the 2007 National Hockey League All-Star SuperSkills Competition, held the night before the All-Star Game.[9] Each of the eight participants was given two opportunities to take a running (skating) start up to the puck and let loose with a fierce slap shot, with only around 15 to 20 seconds separating a player's two attempts (enough time for the player and the measuring instruments to be reset). The speeds of the shots in miles per hour (mph) were revealed instantly on the television broadcast. This hockey competition thus allowed a quantitative look—admittedly from a small sample of players, exhibiting a fairly basic technique—at the reproducibility of a sports action. In 2007, the correlation was near perfect ($r = .88$, where 1.00 is the maximum), indicating that players who really sent the puck zipping along on their first shots also did so on their second shots, whereas those with relatively slow-moving first attempts also attained similar movement on their second shots. For example, the hardest shooter, Zdeno Chara of the Boston Bruins, achieved shot speeds of 99.5 and 100.4 mph, whereas the softest shooter, the New Jersey Devils' Brian Rafalski, recorded marks of 84.6 and 86.8 mph. In this exercise, therefore, slap-shot speed (and presumably the underlying shooting motion) seemed highly reproducible.

Are Our Brains Wired for Consistency?

Though my examination of the NHL "hardest shot" competition suggests that athletes can reproduce basic actions pretty consistently, *exact* duplication of the brain mechanisms needed to perform body movements appears elusive. Thus says Stanford University research (published in the December 21, 2006 issue of *Neuron*) that monitored the brains of rhesus macaque monkeys, as they attempted to carry out various actions. According to a university news release:

> It's as if each time the brain tries to solve the problem of planning how to move, it does it anew. . . . Practice and training can help the brain solve the problem more capably, but people and other primates simply aren't wired for consistency like computers or machines. Instead, people seem to be improvisers by default.[10]

OTHER KINDS OF EVIDENCE FOR STREAKINESS

Though most of the supportive evidence for streakiness appears to be from quickly repeatable, simple motions, a recent study of baseball hitting in major league games—where players must wait perhaps 20 to 30 minutes between at-bats—also appears to provide data consistent with streakiness. The article in question appeared in the 2008 edition of the annual *Baseball Research Journal* from the Society for American Baseball Research (SABR), with the title, "Hitting Streaks Don't Obey Your Rules: Evidence That Hitting Streaks

Aren't Just By-products of Random Variation."[11] Trent McCotter, a Phi Beta Kappa undergraduate at the University of North Carolina–Chapel Hill, and his faculty collaborator Peter Mucha began this project by creating a huge database of year-specific game-by-game hitting data for all players active from 1957 to 2006. Someone who played 10 years would thus have 10 different lines of data. Each line (hypothetically) would look something like the following sequence, where H = getting at least one hit in a game and N = no hits in the game; in reality, however, there would be up to 162 entries for a player, depending on how many games he appeared in:

HHNNN NHNHN . . .

For each player-year, McCotter and Mucha then re-sorted the sequences of H's and N's into some random alternative, such as the following (the number of H's and N's would, of course, be constant between the player's actual sequence and the random re-sorting):

NHNNH NHNNH . . .

In fact, each player-season was randomly re-sorted 10,000 times! McCotter's reasoning was that, if lengthy hitting streaks were simply a result of random variation on a player's underlying hitting ability, the random simulations should produce as many streaks of a given length as actually occurred in a player's real-life hitting portfolio.

The initial results showed the actual frequency of lengthy hitting streaks to be greater than the frequency obtained in the random simulations. For example, 274 actual hitting streaks of 20 or more games occurred in real life, whereas the average of all the excess simulated hitting logs generated 192.43 streaks of that length. For streaks of 25 or more games, 62 actually occurred whereas 35.74 were generated randomly. Similar trends occurred for 30+ and 35+ hitting streaks, although the numbers started to get very small (i.e., 5 streaks of 35 or more games actually occurred in real life, whereas 1.48 were generated randomly).

The greater number of actual, real-life hitting streaks of a given length, relative to the random simulations, is consistent with the idea of a "hot hand" (i.e., a player systematically raising his underlying hitting ability when in the midst of a hot streak), but does not prove the existence of one. As McCotter acknowledges, there could be other reasons for a greater number of lengthy hitting streaks existing than would be expected by chance. For example, a player could be highly aware of his hitting streak and take special action to perpetuate it, such as an aggressive pull-hitter "going with what he's given" and slapping an outside pitch to the opposite field for a single. Also, a hitter may benefit from a generous ruling of "hit" (vs. "error") by the official scorer. (As an aside, a theory of Joe DiMaggio achieving his record 56-game hitting streak *in part* through such generosity has been making the rounds in recent years.[12])

McCotter noted further that his original random simulations included games in which the batter had not started, which could downwardly affect the numbers of streaks in the simulated sequences (i.e., a non-hit game owing to when the batter only appeared once as a pinch-hitter, could insert itself between hit games in the random sequences, thus holding down the length of hitting streaks). A second series of simulations was run, this time excluding non-start games. Indeed, much of the difference between the actual and simulated numbers of streaks disappeared. McCotter describes the following finding, as one example:

> in real life for 1957–2006, there were 274 streaks of 20 or more games; the first permutation (including non-starts) had an average of a mere 192 such streaks; and the second permutation (leaving out non-starts) had an average of 259 such streaks. The difference between 259 and 274 may not sound like much, but it is still very significant when viewed over 10,000 permutations, especially since we still aren't quite comparing apples to apples.[13]

McCotter concluded his article on the following note: "This study shows that sometimes batters really may have a hot hand, or at least that they adapt their approach to try to keep a long hitting streak going—and baseball players are nothing if not adapters."[14]

To the extent McCotter is claiming evidence for a relatively modest-sized hot-hand effect, subject to other possible interpretations, that would not be terribly incompatible with other baseball findings.

What about evidence for streakiness in the sport of basketball? As we'll see later, studies of players' shooting sequences have come down heavily against the idea of hot (or cold) hands. There *is* one type of basketball phenomenon, however, that does appear to suggest the presence of streakiness, and it is the subject of its own brief chapter, appearing next.

4

"We Are a Team of Runs"

Basketball games often appear to be decided by a "run" or "spurt" by one team, in other words, a stretch where one team outscores the other 12–0, 19–2, or by some such lopsided margin. Such a spurt, particularly late in the game, can turn a close contest into a blowout or vice versa. The quote headlining this chapter was made by then–Kansas coach Roy Williams (who later moved to the University of North Carolina) after his Jayhawks' 94–61 win over Marquette in the 2003 NCAA national men's semifinal during the Final Four.[1]

The Marquette game was far from the only tournament game about which Williams could have used the "team of runs" phrase. In Kansas's next outing, the championship game against Syracuse, the Jayhawks nearly overcame an 18-point deficit, falling in a tight finish to the Orange. Still more evidence of Kansas's penchant for going on—and giving up—points in spurts comes from the Jayhawks' two games that season against Arizona. One was a January 25 non-conference match-up in Lawrence, and the other a rematch in the West regional final.

In the first meeting, KU built up a 44–24 first-half lead on many small runs. Arizona then went on an 8–0 run to get within better striking distance, 44–32. A 12–0 run by Arizona closed the Wildcats to within 52–49. Arizona gradually overtook Kansas throughout the second half, and thanks to a 10–0 flourish to end the game, Arizona won 91–74. From being up 20 to losing by 17, of course, the shift constituted a negative 37-point turnaround for the Jayhawks. Kansas got revenge against Arizona in the NCAA tournament, in a game that was no less streak-laden. The Jayhawks led 38–22 in the first half, but the Wildcats closed out the half on a 13–0 run. The Jayhawks countered with an 11–0 run early in the second half, only to have the Wildcats come back shortly thereafter with a 16–0 run. But the Jayhawks ultimately prevailed 78–75.

For Coach Williams to call Kansas a "team of runs" only appears to state the obvious. As is my skeptical nature, however, I felt compelled to check whether the Jayhawks' (and opponents') streaky performances deviated from what could have occurred by chance (i.e., under a model wherein the result of each possession of a basketball game is independent of the previous possession by the same or opposing team). Chance generators (e.g., spinners, computers) cannot experience "momentum," "demoralization," "exhaustion," or other psychological and physical states. Thus, if a chance generator could replicate the spurts observed in actual games, then explanations of spurts that drew upon such psychological states would not be supported. In a manner inspired by Albert and Bennett's aforementioned book *Curve Ball*, I simulated five Kansas-Arizona games using each team's base-rate percentages of scoring 0, 1, 2, or 3 points on a single possession (obtained from the two actual KU-UA games), and a chance generator to determine the points scored on each possession. (Although it is theoretically possible to score more than 3 points on a possession—such as via a made 3-point-shot plus a foul in the act of shooting, or due to technical or intentional fouls—these rare occurrences were omitted for simplicity's sake.) I used the two Kansas-Arizona games as the foundation for the simulation base rates for two reasons: (a) each team's base rate would be in relation to the one specific opponent, and (b) averaging together the statistics from two games would presumably add reliability to the base rates.

A possession was defined as basically "a trip down the court." A single possession could involve a fair amount of action (e.g., a missed shot, offensive rebound, and then put-back). The idea of breaking the game down possession by possession is one I got from Tim Chambers, who at the end of Texas Tech basketball radio broadcasts, announces a statistic he calls the "Offensive Efficiency Rating," which is basically each team's points per possession.[2] What I did was a little different. Counting each possession of each team and how many points a given team scored on the possession, I arrived at the following table for the Jayhawks and Wildcats:

Table 4.1

Points	Proportion of the Time for KU	KU Spinner Numbers	Proportion of the Time for UA	UA Spinner Numbers
0	.54	1–54	.49	1–49
1	.04	55–58	.05	50–54
2	.30	59–88	.34	55–88
3	.12	89–100	.12	89–100

The table tells us that on 54 percent of its possessions in the two games against Arizona (combined), Kansas came away with no points (this reflects more than just shooting percentage, as a team could get a zero-point possession by turning the ball over without ever having taken a shot). Further, on 4 percent of its possessions the Jayhawks came away with 1 point, on 30 percent they came away with 2 points, and on 12 percent, 3 points. Similar breakdowns are shown for Arizona, based on the Wildcats' two games against Kansas.

Each possession in the five simulated games had its scoring outcome determined via a random-number generator (http://www.randomizer.org). To begin, I requested a series of numbers from 1 to 100. Because 54 percent of the time Kansas scored no points on a possession, whenever a random number from 1 to 54 appeared, it was scored as no points for the Jayhawks in the simulated games (see table 4.1). Following the above percentages, a random number from 55 to 58 (representing 4 percent) was taken as 1 point for KU, and so forth. Arizona had its own scoring legend (also shown in table 4.1) to interpret its random numbers that were generated.

In the NCAA tournament game between the Jayhawks and Wildcats, each team had 75 possessions, whereas in the mid-season game, Arizona had 77 and Kansas 78. It thus seemed reasonable to (roughly) average the number of possessions from the two actual KU-UA games and conduct the simulations with 76 possessions per team. For the five simulated games, I alternated which team got the first possession. Given that Arizona had a bigger aggregate margin of victory over the two real games between the teams, it should come as no surprise that Arizona "won" all five of the simulated games (although that was of much lesser import than the spurts).

Table 4.2 shows a sample sequence from one of the simulated games; Kansas drew random number 65 in its first possession, worth two points, followed by Arizona drawing number 39, for no points. KU then drew number 37 for its second possession (worth no points), and so forth. The depicted sequence illustrates an 8–0 Arizona run (see point values in *italics,* starting with an Arizona 2, followed by a Kansas 0, then another Arizona 2, etc.).

Table 4.2

Kansas		Arizona	
Random No.	Points	Random No.	Points
65	2	39	0
37	0	56	2
31	0	74	2
47	0	70	2
12	0	85	2
96	3	52	1

In defining what I thought was a noteworthy run, I decided on 7–0 or greater; I only used spurts in which one team completely shut out the other, although one could also include non–shut-out runs such as 13–1 or 23–4. Because a 6–0 run could simply be the product of a three-pointer, one defensive stop, and another 3, I wanted something beyond 6–0. I obtained the following runs in the simulated games:

GAME 1	GAME 2	GAME 3	GAME 4	GAME 5
Arizona 8–0	Arizona 7–0	Arizona 9–0	Arizona 7–0	None
Arizona 7–0	Kansas 7–0	Arizona 10–0	Kansas 9–0	
	Arizona 7–0	Kansas 7–0		
	Arizona 7–0	Arizona 7–0		

Overall, 12 shut-out runs of 7–0 or greater were observed in the five simulated games, for an average of 2.4 per game. The *frequency* of these runs seemed pretty comparable to those observed in the actual KU-UA games. However, the *magnitude levels* of the runs were largely higher in the actual games (e.g., 11–0, 12–0, 13–0, and 16–0) than in the simulations of chance/independence.

The very small size of this study dictates caution in interpreting the results. However, the results do suggest that runs or spurts observed in actual games may be more potent than those derived from a chance simulation, thus supporting concepts such as momentum and demoralization. Another consideration, however, is that runs in actual games may involve one team's star player missing a prolonged period of time due to injury or foul trouble. Assuming the player excelled both offensively and defensively, his (or her) absence would probably make the point-scoring base rates different for both teams during the stretch in question than base rates derived from two full games.

Further research, with larger numbers of games and simulations and teams representing a wider range of abilities than just the elite Kansas and Arizona squads, would be welcome.

Results from this line of inquiry would also seem to have implications for the strategy of calling a time-out in the early stages of an opponent's run in an attempt to stop the opponent's apparent momentum and minimize the damage from the run. If runs are ultimately shown to follow a pattern fully consistent with chance and independence, then time-outs designed to stop them would appear to be irrelevant. But, if there turns out to be something more than chance to team runs, the strategy of calling time-outs *may* be valid (we won't know until further research is done that focuses specifically on time-outs).

Born to Run

During the 2004 NCAA men's basketball tournament, I made it a point to check articles and play-by-play sheets to estimate the prevalence of major runs (defined generally as outscoring an opponent by at least 10 points, with the opponent scoring very few points). Nearly three-quarters of the games (47 out of 64) featured at least one major run. They are listed here (teams listed as going on the run won the game, unless noted otherwise).

ROUND OF 64, DAY ONE

- UConn 12–0 run against Vermont
- UTEP 13–2 run in missed comeback vs. Maryland
- Stanford 12–0 run against Texas–San Antonio
- Texas (24–6 run) prevents Princeton (12–0 run) upset
- North Carolina ends game on 25–8 run against Air Force
- Seton Hall 23–5 run against Arizona
- Duke 12–0 run against Alabama St.
- Texas Tech 14–0 run against Charlotte
- Gonzaga 12–2 run against Valparaiso
- Nevada closes game on 16–3 run to beat Michigan State (who earlier had 15–0 run)

ROUND OF 64, DAY TWO

- Wisconsin has 34–8 run against Richmond (Badgers also score on 20 straight possessions during the spurt)
- Vanderbilt 16–2 run against Western Michigan
- Mississippi State 22–5 run against Monmouth
- Xavier 36–10 run against Louisville
- Cincinnati opens game 11–0 against East Tennessee St.

(continued on next page)

Born to Run *(continued from previous page)*

- Illinois 10–0 run against Murray State
- Oklahoma State has two second-half runs (12–2 and 14–2) against Eastern Washington
- Memphis 13–2 run against South Carolina
- Georgia Tech (30–8 run) defeats Northern Iowa (who had 27–9 run)
- Kansas 21–2 run against Illinois-Chicago
- Alabama–Birmingham (19–9 and 16–1 runs) against Washington
- Kentucky 15–2 run against Florida A&M

ROUND OF 32, DAY ONE

- St. Joseph's 24–2 run against Texas Tech
- Alabama 16–0 run against Stanford
- UConn 16–2 run against DePaul
- Syracuse 10–0 run against Maryland

ROUND OF 32, DAY TWO

- Vanderbilt and NC State trade runs: Vandy opens up game 16–4, NC State goes on 15–2 run midway through game, Vandy gets late 10–0 run to win
- Kansas and Pacific trade runs: KU 15–2 first-half spurt countered by UOP 12–0 run, but Jayhawks' 15–3 second-half run proves decisive
- Oklahoma State and Memphis trade runs: OSU gets early 12–1 run, Memphis attempts rally later with 23–9 run, but comes up short
- Alabama–Birmingham and Kentucky trade runs: UAB gets early 18–5 run, Kentucky fights back later with 11–0 blitz, but to no avail
- Wisconsin's 12–2 run in losing to Pittsburgh
- Mississippi State opens game 23–13, but Xavier rebounds with 21–10 run to win
- Illinois defeats Cincinnati with early (17–5) and late (13–2) runs
- Georgia Tech 18–6 run against Boston College

ROUND OF 16, DAY ONE

- UConn takes early control over Vanderbilt with 17–1 run, survives 16–3 Commodore comeback attempt
- Oklahoma State 17–5 run against Pitt
- St. Joseph's 13–1 run against Wake Forest
- Alabama's 19–5 run against Syracuse

ROUND OF 16, DAY TWO

- Kansas opens game 18–6, has late 12–0 run against Alabama-Birmingham
- Xavier 10–0 run against Texas
- Georgia Tech 17–6 run against Nevada

ROUND OF 8, DAY ONE

- UConn 17–4 run against Alabama
- Oklahoma State 14–2 run against St. Joseph's

ROUND OF 8, DAY TWO

- Georgia Tech's two runs (11–0 early in game, 13–3 in overtime) against KU

FINAL 4 (NATIONAL SEMIFINALS)

- Georgia Tech 15–4 run against Oklahoma State
- UConn versus Duke features several runs (UConn opens game with 15–4 run, ultimately wins game thanks to late 12–0 run); Duke has first half 30–9 spurt

FINAL GAME

- UConn dominates with 30–14 run to close first half and 13–3 run early in second half. Georgia Tech's 21–9 run in closing minutes too little, too late.

5

Evidence Against a Hot Hand: Basketball

"Like all good shooters, when you give him open looks they find the rim," he said. *"And once you let a good shooter find the rim, it's over. I don't care how hard you guard him after that, every time he lets it go it's going in."*

—Kansas State men's basketball coach Frank Martin, after Texas Tech's Alan Voskuil went five for six from behind the three-point arc in the Red Raiders' 2008 upset win over the Wildcats[1]

Coach Martin is far from the only basketball observer to believe in the "hot hand." Gilovich, Vallone, and Tversky—mentioned in chapter 2 as launching the field of hot hand research—conducted a survey of college-student basketball fans and intramural players regarding belief in the hot hand, and found that 91 percent of respondents agreed with the notion of a player having "a better chance of making a shot after having just made his last two or three shots than he does after having just missed his last two or three shots."[2] This finding set the stage for Gilovich and colleagues to conduct their studies of actual shooting statistics to see if the observers' beliefs had any validity. The findings of these studies will be discussed shortly. The research reviewed two chapters ago, which focused on relatively simple athletic performance tasks such as bowling and golf putting (on a course laid out in a laboratory), tended to show support for streakiness. What about more complex, game-type situations—such as in basketball, where a shooter must contend with defenders, or baseball hitting (covered in the following chapter), where the ball is not stationary, but is instead delivered by pitchers who are expert in the fastball and curveball?

As noted, Gilovich, Vallone, and Tversky inquired into the possible streakiness of basketball shooting. These researchers first looked at personal shot sequences for nine members of the 1980–81 Philadelphia 76ers. It turned out that these players' probabilities of hitting a shot given an immediately prior *hit* were uncannily similar to their probabilities of hitting a shot given an immediately prior *miss*. Nor were players' hit rates higher after just making their last *three* shots than after just missing their last three shots (note that this finding is opposite of what Dorsey-Palmateer and Smith found with bowling, as reported previously).[3] All in all, this was bad news for the notion of a hot hand!

Real-time basketball game data are "noisy" for a number of reasons, however, such as players' varying the distances of their shot attempts and the presence of defenders. A player who has just made a shot may feel extra confidence and attempt his or her next one from further away, thus diminishing the chances of detecting a hot hand. Further, the opposing team may attempt to defend a shooter more closely after he or she has made a few shots in a row. Additional studies by Gilovich and colleagues that attempted to get around these problems by using free-throw data and shooting sessions in the gymnasium (where the researchers could control the distances and other aspects of the shooting experience) likewise came up empty in the search for a hot hand, however.

For nearly a quarter century following the studies of Gilovich and colleagues, other researchers continued to look for evidence of streaky shooting in professional basketball, using other venues such as the NBA three-point-shooting contest held each year in conjunction with the All-Star Game. To the best of my knowledge, no study has found evidence of a hot hand in basketball. A common criticism of Gilovich's and others' studies are their small sample sizes, which make it difficult to detect statistically significant patterns of streakiness. Over the years, however, with the spread of internet access to detailed basketball play-by-play sheets and other statistical information, it seemed inevitable that ever more thorough studies could, and would, be conducted.[4]

In 2009, John Huizinga and Sandy Weil presented a study that goes a long way toward fulfilling the promise of voluminous data. Claiming "over 200 times as much data" as Gilovich and colleagues, and the ability to incorporate "game-contextual information," Huizinga and Weil set out in search of evidence for streakiness or its opposite, negative dependencies (i.e., where making one shot tends to be followed by *missing* the next).[5] Analyses were limited to only the most "prolific" shooters in the NBA from 2002–03 to 2005–06, which generally meant that a player attempted at least 1,500 shots per season.

Players who qualified for analysis included Kobe Bryant, LeBron James, and other prominent names; in the words of ESPN.com's Henry Abbott, who commented on the Huizinga-Weil study, "on the face of it, it's a no-brainer that if anyone in the NBA has been hot, these players are it."[6] Regarding the game-contextual information noted above, Huizinga and Weil utilized statistical techniques that could take into account factors including shot distance; opponents' defensive quality; whether a given possession arises from an in-bounds play (which gives the defense a chance to set up) or from a "live-ball" situation such as a turnover or rebound; and whether a given game is at home or away for the focal player. Huizinga and Weil's major findings were as follows:

- "Our subjects average 46.7% field goal shooting after any missed shot but it drops to 43.2% after a made jump shot."[7] (They also studied non–jump shots, such as lay-ups and dunks, but results for these were weaker and probably of lesser interest to most observers. A crowd gets excited when a player makes several straight from long distance, not when it's from right under the basket.)

- Making shots from longer distance (i.e., jumpers) appeared to lead to a player being more likely to take his next shot from a longer distance than if he had missed a longer shot. In general, the players in the study took 23.7 percent of their shots from short distance (i.e., non-jumpers). Making a jumper reduced players' likelihood of taking their next shot from close in to 15 percent.

- Nailing a jump shot seemed to make players want to shoot again more quickly than if they had missed: "After a missed jump shot, the player takes about 56.5 seconds of team possession time on average to take his next shot. After a made jump shot, he takes only 47.3 seconds."[8]

In short, Huizinga and Weil found no evidence of a hot hand (i.e., that making a shot raises players' success rate on the next attempt), but, in fact, found evidence against it. There is some suggestion in the data that players believed in the hot hand, however, as hitting a shot appeared to increase their readiness to take their next shot from farther away, and more quickly, than usual.

Beyond actual game data, another favorite venue for testing the hot hand hypothesis has been the NBA All-Star Game three-point shooting contests. Jay Koehler and Caryn Conley published an article on the topic, and I've conducted a number of my own unpublished analyses. In a given round (i.e., preliminary, semifinals, finals) each player attempts 25 shots along the three-point arc, five each from five different locations (far right-hand corner;

Should Basketball Teams Pass the Ball to Someone Who Has Made His or Her Last Few Shots?

If, as appears to be the case, a player making one or more consecutive shots does not raise his or her probability of making the next shot (beyond his or her typical success rate), then the strategy of passing the ball to a player on a hot streak would seem to have no benefit.

Not so fast. Bruce Burns points out, for one thing, that players who exhibit streaks of hot shooting also tend to have high shooting percentages.[9] Thus, passing the ball to a shooter on a hot streak will mean that the ball is getting into the hands of a good overall shooter. In the NBA, a team's coach and players would presumably be well versed in each player's strengths and weaknesses as a shooter, so a short-term streak by someone might not be that informative.

On the other hand, notes Burns, "players in a pick-up game of basketball who do not know each other may gain a greater advantage for their team by using streaks as an allocation cue than would NBA players who know their teammates well."[10] Though the details are beyond the scope of this book, Burns has extensive calculations and computer simulations to back up his claim that passing the ball to a hot shooter should result in a team scoring more points than doing otherwise.

halfway between that corner and the top of the key; top of the key; halfway toward the left-hand corner; and far left-hand corner). Not only does the NBA three-point contest hold the distance of the shot constant; as Koehler and Conley note, the atmosphere at the event approximates actual NBA action through the inclusion of "professional players, competition, high stakes, professional court, and a large crowd and television audience."[11] Koehler and Conley examined the shooting sequences from 23 players in NBA three-point contests from 1994 to 1997 (somewhat artificially, as these authors acknowledged, they "tied together" multiple 25-shot sequences for each player in chronological order, even though there could be long separations between rounds). Koehler and Conley found very little evidence of streaky shooting. Only 2 out of the 23 players had appreciably fewer runs than would be expected by chance. Tests of the "p-hit-hit" type (introduced in chapter 2) similarly failed to support a hot hand. My unpublished studies from the 1998, 2000, and 2002 NBA three-point contests have also found little support for a hot hand; out of the many 25-shot sequences completed each year, perhaps *one* shows solid evidence of a hot hand.

Koehler and Conley did something else, however, that was quite fascinating. From their videotapes of the contests, they took note of announcers' spontaneous exclamations that a player was on a hot streak during his sequence of attempts (e.g., "Legler is on fire!" in reference to former Washington Wizards player Tim Legler). If one accepts that attaining "hotness" means that a player should hit his (or her) next shots with a higher-than-usual probability, then Koehler and Conley's results are disappointing for the notion of streakiness. Players hit 53.9 percent of their shots overall in the contests; immediately after the announcers' hotness outbursts, where we would expect a much higher hit rate, the players made their shots at only a slightly higher clip, 55.2 percent. Immediately *before* the exclamations, of course, 86.2 percent of the shots had gone in—the announcers thus accurately reflected what *had been* happening, but their statements had no predictive value.

Relativity Theory

After videotaping and watching the televised coverage of the 2002 contest, I noticed an interesting exchange among two of the commentators, former players Kenny Smith and Charles Barkley. Smith had made a comment regarding continuity of motion (which from our perspective harks back to a couple of chapters ago). After each shot, contestants must reach back and grab another ball from a rack, which Smith contended could disrupt players' shooting process. Here is the exchange:

SMITH: See, the uncomfortable thing is that, normally when you see this many shots, someone's throwing you the ball. Now you're reaching back away from your normal body rhythm. That's probably the biggest thing that I felt.

BARKLEY: You sure make a lot of excuses. Somebody... it's not uncomfortable for somebody, because somebody win[s] it every year.

Sir Charles, in this instance, is not recognizing the distinction between *relative* success, which necessitates that indeed *somebody* will win, and *absolute* success, where the factor identified by Smith could be harming *all* the players' performances. Smith, however, was thinking along the right lines, in my view, just like a theorist of the hot hand.

In summary, the overwhelming majority of players, across a number of studies, have not shown evidence of a hot hand. Claims of streaky shooting instead appear to be only anecdotal. To close our review of basketball evidence, I thought it would be fun to look at one such isolated case of a player who appeared to exhibit streak shooting during one season. This player is Ohio State University's Je'Kel Foster (isn't that a perfect name for someone who goes hot and cold in his shooting, akin to the shifts in personality of the literary character Dr. Jekyll/Mr. Hyde?). In the middle-late part of Big Ten play in 2006, Foster had an amazingly hot stretch on three-point shots, followed by an equally astonishing cold stretch. Take a look at this lovely graph from the website Buckeye Commentary, shown here as figure 5.1, which illustrates his game-by-game three-point shooting percentages in a chronological sequence of games against conference opponents (with one non-conference game, against Florida A&M, mixed in).[12]

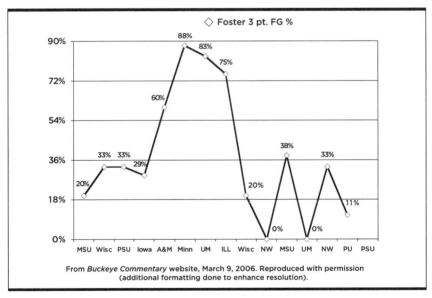

Figure 5.1

What you'll see is that Foster was consistently shooting (roughly) at a mind-boggling *80 percent* clip on three-point attempts during a three-game stretch (against opponents Minnesota, Michigan/UM, and Illinois). This was then followed by a six-game stint in which his average three-point percentage was in the teens! Given Foster's 40 percent overall success rate from behind the arc that season, it certainly appears that his top performances were better than what would be expected by chance, and his low points lower.

6

Evidence Against a Hot Hand: Baseball

Baseball hitting in real games is another task whose success or failure would appear to be heavily dependent on the environmental context—the quality of the pitcher, whether the batter's swing is of the same or opposite handedness as the pitcher's throwing arm, whether it's a night or day game (which may affect the ball's visibility to the batter), etc. As discussed previously, factors affecting the simplicity or complexity of a task are likely to hold critical importance for streakiness. Sixteen years before Huizinga and Weil's enormous study of basketball shooting, Chris Albright did something similar for baseball, taking a variety of situational factors into account in testing for streakiness of success in hitters' at-bats. For each player in a given year (e.g., former Red Sox outfielder Dwight Evans in 1988), Albright conducted what is known as a logistic regression analysis. Looking at a player's overall portfolio of at-bats in a particular season, the question was whether the outcome of the current at-bat (success or failure, with hits, walks, and sacrifices counting as successes, and outs as failures) was statistically associated with the outcome of the *previous* at-bat. Streak-hitting would be evident if there were a higher probability of success following a successful at-bat, than following an unsuccessful one (it's the same "p(hit | hit)" vs. "p(hit | miss)" comparison discussed previously). The key, however, was taking into account pitcher quality and aspects of game environment.[1]

Steven Levitt and Stephen Dubner, whose 2005 book *Freakonomics* has probably done more than any other recent publication to bring statistical analysis to the general public, describe regression techniques as tools that "artificially [hold] constant every variable except the two [the researcher] wishes to focus on, and then [show] how those two co-vary."[2] Specifically, the variables that Albright held constant statistically included the earned run average (ERA) of

36

the pitcher faced in a given at-bat, pitcher's handedness, home/away status of the game for the batter, and night/day status. By holding these factors constant (i.e., removing their influence) across huge numbers of data points, any findings that linked the outcome of a given at-bat with the outcome of the previous at-bat can more readily be interpreted as a momentum effect. Alternative interpretations, for example, that the batter faced an unusually easy pitcher in one game and thus got four straight hits due to pitcher weakness rather than inherent streakiness on the part of the batter, could thus be ruled out.

Albright found that, indeed, there were *some* batters in *some* seasons who showed evidence of streak hitting. One example is the aforementioned Dwight Evans in 1988. His batting average was .124 higher after a success than after a failure. However, evidence of streaky player seasons was very rare. As Albright noted, "there are generally about as many statistically significant [findings] as one would expect from a randomness model."[3] Albright had multiple seasons of data for each player, so it was possible to test whether players who showed evidence of streakiness in one season also showed it in other seasons. The claim that a player is by *nature* a streak hitter (or streak shooter in basketball) would seem to require that the player be able to repeat his (or her) streaky performance of one season in additional seasons. Yet, of the 40 players for whom four years of data were available, *none* exhibited consistent year-to-year streakiness. Albright's article was followed within the same 1993 issue of the *Journal of the American Statistical Association* (JASA) by commentaries from other prominent statisticians, with Albright providing a rejoinder at the end. Interested readers are invited to look at the commentaries in JASA.

The 2001 publication of the book *Curve Ball* by academic statistician Jim Albert and his colleague from private industry, Jay Bennett, opened my eyes to another valuable method of hot hand research, namely the computer simulation (a variation of which of I used in chapter 4 in my simulated college basketball games between Kansas and Arizona). Whereas the rigorous study of statistics can involve logarithms, calculus, and other advanced mathematical concepts, Albert and Bennett were able to illustrate their points using a children's board game! Another step taken by Albert and Bennett was to focus less on batters' exact sequences—at-bat by at-bat—and to look instead at daily hitting performance; hypothetically, three-for-four would be a good day, regardless of the exact sequence, and one-for-five would be a bad day.[4]

Oft-traveled infielder Todd Zeile had a reputation as a streaky hitter, according to Albert and Bennett, so they focused on him, plotting Zeile's day-to-day moving average of batting performances over the first half of the 1999

Maybe It's Streak Pitching

Like the NBA and NHL, Major League Baseball hosts a skills competition on the eve of its all-star game, the Home Run Derby. Each batter, having brought a personally chosen batting-practice pitcher, tries to hit as many homers as he can before recording 10 "outs" (an out being a swing that results in anything other than a home run). I analyzed the 2001 and 2002 Home Run Derbies for streakiness and found that only one or two batters per year showed signs of streak hitting. The shortness of the hitting sequences arguably makes the limited amount of streaky home-run hitting somewhat impressive, as small sample sizes make it harder to obtain statistically significant results. On the other hand, some observers have noted that what looks like streak hitting might really be as much or more a manifestation of "streak pitching," where the batter's partner on the mound keeps putting the ball in the same place for the batter to swat. In 2008, the Texas Rangers' Josh Hamilton hit a single-round record 28 homers during one of his trips to the plate, including 13 in a row. In fact, 71-year-old Clay Counsil, who used to pitch batting practice to Hamilton when the latter was a high-schooler, reprised this role in the Derby and seemed particularly adept at consistently putting the ball in the same location for Hamilton.[5] From there, Hamilton's beautiful swing did the rest.

---

season (an artistic rendering with an appearance not unlike a plot of the stock market's ups and downs). Sure enough, Zeile appeared to exhibit both pronounced "hot" performances (a batting average over .500 for one stretch of games) and "cold" ones (a stretch where his average dipped below .100).

The question, again, is whether this pattern deviates from what could occur by chance within a fairly long sequence. To address this question, Albert and Bennett invoked the aforementioned children's board game, "All-Star Baseball." Many of you, provided you're of a certain age, will recall this pre-videogame activity, in which circular cardboard disks representing each player are inserted into spinners to determine the result of any at-bat. The outer edge of each spinner disk is divided into sections representing different possible outcomes of an at-bat (e.g., home run, single, strike-out), with the size of each section proportional to that player's lifetime relative frequency of obtaining that outcome. In other words, if a player had a lifetime frequency of homering in 10 percent of his plate appearances, 10 percent of the circle (or 36 degrees) would represent home runs. The bigger the section, the greater would be the probability of the spinner ending up there.

To simplify matters, Albert and Bennett created a "Zeile spinner" with just two zones: "hit" (equal to .280 of the spinner area, based on Zeile's past performances) and "out" (equal to .720 of area). Now, if we spin this same spinner repeatedly, we *know* that his true probability of getting a hit is .280 on every spin; in other words, the underlying model is of Zeile as a consistent hitter. Next, Albert and Bennett "spun" their .280 spinner (they actually used a computer to simulate doing so) to replicate Zeile's game performances. For example, because Todd Zeile, the real person, had four at-bats in his first game of the 1999 season, the researchers spun their spinner four times, and so forth for all games included in the simulation. The results of this simulation were absolutely fascinating. Even though the spinner had a consistent .280 hit percentage (by definition), the simulated spins generated similar sequences of peaks and valleys in batting average to what the real Zeile had obtained. Thus, just as a coin with a known true probability of .50 heads and .50 tails can by chance yield "wild" patterns in short sequences (e.g., 9 heads and 1 tail), a simulated hitter (the spinner) programmed to have a consistent .280 probability of a hit on each "at-bat" can exhibit pronounced hot and cold streaks.

To a large extent, then, the real Zeile's patterns of hot and cold streakiness are compatible with him truly being a *consistent* hitter. The peaks and valleys would just be due to chance. I should note that I have somewhat oversimplified Albert and Bennett's analyses, to keep the discussion focused. There were also some indications that Zeile's reputation as a streaky hitter would not necessarily be off the mark, based on more complex spinner models to test for streakiness. Albert and Bennett's conclusion, however, was as follows: "Generally, while some players may exhibit some streaky batting behavior, one should be pretty doubtful of labeling someone a streaky hitter. Chance is a very powerful force in creating streaks."[6]

Albert has continued to search for the hot bat, most recently with a 2008 article.[7] In it, he used data from the 2005 MLB season to investigate various streakiness-related questions. In his brief overview, Albert concludes: "[An] exchangeable model that assumes that all players are consistent with constant probabilities of success appears to explain much of the observed streaky behavior. . . . A player who appears unusually streaky in hits doesn't generally appear streaky in strikeouts and home runs."[8]

Another statistically oriented baseball volume, *The Book: Playing the Percentages in Baseball*, by Tom Tango, Mitchel Lichtman, and Andy Dolphin, provides

A More Recent Example

To get a more recent example, I replicated the Zeile analysis with April–May 2009 statistics for the New York Mets' David Wright. In a June 1 posting, blogger Matthew Cerrone characterized Wright as a streaky hitter, and indeed the Mets' third-baseman had pronounced periods of hotness and coldness during the first two months of the '09 season.[9] The question is whether repeated spins of a spinner whose "hit area" was constantly one-third (matching Wright's batting average during April and May of .333) could generate similar ups and downs in Wright's batting average to what the real Wright exhibited. Results of the Wright batting simulation are shown in the following graph, where rises well above .333 are indicative of hot streaks and falls well below .333 represent cold streaks.

David Wright's Batting Average (Four-Game Moving Average) from Early Months of 2009 Season, Actual and Simulated from a Constant .333 Spinner

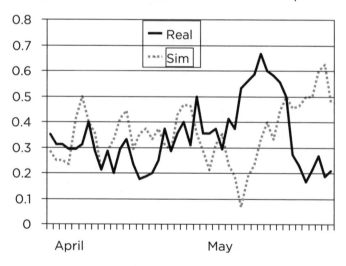

Indeed, the spinner simulation with each at-bat always carrying a .333 probability of a hit (making Wright a true consistent hitter), was able to reproduce stretches of extreme hotness (a .600 spurt near the end of the sequence) and coldness (a dip below .100 in early May), purely via random fluctuations from a model of consistency.

a streak-hitting analysis.[10] If there really is something to the idea of a hot bat beyond just random fluctuation—that is, a player *really* is in a prolonged state of seeing the ball or timing his swing better than usual—then we would expect hot streaks of some specified length (*The Book* used five games) to be followed by better-than-usual hitting (and the same reasoning to apply to cold streaks). As ably summarized by Dave Cameron on the Seattle baseball blog *U.S.S. Mariner*:

> To test this, they pulled in every play from the 2000 to 2003 seasons and identified hot and cold streaks as the upper and lower 5% of all performances over any five-game sample that included at least 20 plate appearances. . . . That gave them 543 unique players creating a total of 6,408 "hot streaks," and 633 players creating a total of 6,489 cold streaks. . . . For offensive performance, they use a metric called Weighted On Base Average, of [*sic*] wOBA for short, which essentially sums up total offensive performance and scales it to look like on-base percentage. . . . The production of the hitters in their sixth game after being identified as being hot [was found to be] .004 better than expected if we had just used a three-year average of their past performance and had no knowledge of what they'd done in their previous five games. Statistically significant? Yes, but by the thinnest of margins. . . . The result [was] basically the same on the opposite end—the players performed worse than expected by an ever so tiny margin immediately after a five-game super slump.[11]

In research involving large samples of games, conducted by different investigators, and looking at different seasons, evidence of streak hitting thus appears hard to come by. For readers seeking further discussion of this topic, I would recommend the chapter "Streaks and Slumps" in Mike Stadler's 2007 book *The Psychology of Baseball*.

TEAM STREAKINESS

Day-to-day hitting is, of course, not the only possible manifestation of a hot hand in baseball. Pitching—consecutive strikeouts or scoreless innings, for example—and fielding—consecutive chances without an error—could also be studied from the statistical perspective of streakiness. Or, one could try to put all of the component skills together and look at team winning and losing streaks. Albert and Bennett did just that, examining all 30 MLB teams in the 1998 season to see how many of them exhibited streakiness, compared to what

Whether George Brett and Tony Gwynn Were Streaky Hitters

One of my proudest moments in the history of the Hot Hand website occurred in 2005, when the legendary baseball statistician Bill James sent me (with permission to publish them) some analyses he had done of possible streakiness in the career hitting records of two Hall of Fame players, George Brett and Tony Gwynn.[12] A major part of James's essay had to do with developing a measure of *instantaneous* hotness or coldness. The traditional measure of batting average is "conservative" in picking up changes in how a hitter is doing; hypothetically, if a player had been batting .250 based on 75 hits in 300 at-bats, going five-for-five in the next game would raise his average only to .262. Instead, James came up with a formula for what he called hitting "temperature," which he described as "a deliberately unstable measure of hitting ability, designed to swing relatively freely based on the player's most recent performance." James then compared how markedly Brett and Gwynn's temperatures for batting average and slugging percentage swung up and down over their careers, relative to randomly generated sequences. James concluded that he had found some evidence of hot hands (or, more technically, nonrandom clustering of hot and cold stretches) among these star hitters, but that it was "not overwhelming."

could be expected by chance. These authors defined team streakiness to reflect the combination of: (a) the amount of time, and (b) the degree, to which a given team's winning percentage hovered above and/or below its overall (season-end) winning percentage as the season progressed. Findings showed that the number of teams exhibiting streakiness in 1998 exceeded what would be expected by chance, but not by that much.[13]

Another question relating to streakiness and momentum is whether playoff-bound MLB teams that finish the regular season on a "hot" note are more likely to do well in the post-season than are teams that "limp" into the playoffs. The 2007 Colorado Rockies would probably come to mind for many baseball fans as a team that indeed rode the wave of a scintillating close to the regular season through two playoff rounds to make the World Series. Different authors have written on this issue, with the analysis by Dave Studeman of the *Hardball Times* perhaps being the most detailed. Writing in September 2005, Studeman looked at every playoff team from 1969 to 2004 (prior to 1969, the teams with the best records in the National and American Leagues went directly into the World Series, with no preliminary playoff rounds; also note that there was no post-season play in 1994 due to the players' strike). Of particular interest to Studeman were teams' overall regular-season win-loss records (which he referred to as teams' "Good" factor) and their records during the final month of the regular season, September (the "Momentum" factor). Here's what I considered the key finding: "In about half of the last 35 years (17, to be exact), the team with the best regular-season record was also the team with the best record in September. Of those 17 teams, six won the World Series. Even teams that were Good and had Momentum won it all only 35% of the time."[14] There are, of course, also anecdotes that reinforce the idea of September momentum being unimportant. Writing in October 2006, David Henderson and Charles Hooper pointed out that the two teams in that year's World Series, the St. Louis Cardinals and the Detroit Tigers, each had some dreadful losing stretches as the regular season came to a close.[15]

CONCLUSION

Whether looking at hitting in real games, the annual Home Run Derby slugging exhibitions, or team winning/losing stretches, statistical studies tend to come up with little or no evidence for true streakiness (i.e., previous success raising a hitter's or team's probability of success in their next attempts) or momentum. A large number of conditions beyond the batter's underlying hitting ability factor into the outcome of even a single at-bat (e.g., pitcher quality, fielders' quality, weather conditions). Once we start talking about entire games, we must consider and integrate the contributions of the nine (or more) players who take the field for a team, the quality of the opposition, whether a team is tired due to extensive travel, etc. In short, the lack of support for baseball streakiness should not be a surprise. Dan Spencer, the baseball coach at my home university, Texas Tech, appeared to be on the right track when he emphasized the importance of the pitcher a team sends out to the mound: "Momentum is your next starter."[16]

Like virtually all research, the studies purporting to show a lack of evidence for the hot hand must be interpreted with some degree of caution. The aforementioned Bill James, in a 2004 article entitled "Underestimating the Fog," listed several conclusions baseball researchers had reached over the years. As three examples, researchers had concluded that there was little or no evidence for: batters' maintaining clutch-hitting ability from one year to the next; streaky hitting; and "protection" in baseball batting orders (i.e., the present batter being helped by having a good hitter behind him). What James argued, however, was that the failure to find statistically significant support for the above phenomena does *not* mean that they do not exist.[17] It may just be that our sample sizes have not been large enough or our measurements not precise enough. In other words, there may be a lot of "fog" out there—as he put it—obscuring our analyses.

Thus, future studies with better methods conceivably could find support for some of the phenomena. Readers with statistical training may recognize in James's words the concept of "statistical power." According to a UCLA statistical analysis website, "Power is the probability of detecting an effect, given that the effect is really there," and the best-known way to increase statistical power is to increase one's sample size.[18] To the argument that we might be able to detect a heretofore undetected phenomenon if only we had a larger sample size, the counter is that a phenomenon that needs a large sample to be detected is probably fairly weak. I think James's skepticism may go a little too far, but I highly recommend his article for its thought-provoking arguments. For readers interested in further discussion of evidence for and against the hot hand, more technical, academic summaries have been published by Michael Bar-Eli and colleagues and An Oskarsson and colleagues.[19]

Momentum Builders or Killers?

Certain kinds of plays have a reputation for either launching or killing a team's momentum. In baseball, a lead-off walk supposedly is an impetus for the hitting team to have a big inning, more so than if the lead-off batter made it to first via a single (perhaps because a walk conveys a lack of pitcher sharpness). On the other hand, in no-out situations, a double-play is supposedly more of a momentum-killer for the batting team than would be two outs made individually by two different batters (holding constant the number of runners remaining on base with two outs). Rebecca Sela and Jeffrey Simonoff conducted extensive statistical analyses of baseball play-by-play data to see if certain outcomes of at-bats indeed enhanced or depressed the offensive team's prospects of getting hits and scoring runs on the immediately following at-bats.[20] Another word for statistical dependency between consecutive at-bats is, of course, *momentum*. Overall, these authors found the evidence for momentum to be "weak, if not nonexistent."[21] The conventional wisdom on lead-off walks (vs. lead-off singles) was not supported. However, Sela and Simonoff's rigorous statistical tests found double-plays truly to be demoralizing and debilitating to teams' offensive production.

7

Revisiting Golf (Briefly)

As readers will recall from chapter 3, golf putting in the controlled environment of a laboratory has produced some evidence of streakiness. When examining player performance levels during actual competitions on authentic golf courses, however, researchers face a number of complexities. First, unlike singular tasks such as rolling a bowling ball or shooting a free-throw in basketball, competitive golf requires each player to master very different kinds of swings (i.e., driving, chipping, putting). Second, golf holes vary in their difficulty, both within and between tournaments. Even using holes' *par* designations (i.e., the number of strokes in which players are expected to hit the ball in the hole) to control for hole difficulty—which many researchers have done—is an imperfect solution. Two holes could have the same par value (say, par 3), yet in practice, one hole could take more strokes on average for players in the field to make, than does the other.

The most active investigator of golf streakiness in actual competitive tournaments appears to be psychology professor Russell Clark of the University of North Texas. Clark has published at least twelve articles on the statistical analysis of professional golf data, on streakiness as well as 'choking.' In studying streakiness, Clark has examined both hole-to-hole and round-to-round continuity (or lack thereof) in golfers' successful outcomes. The following two studies are illustrative of Clark's research. In one study, using a hole-to-hole approach, Clark defined success as a birdie or better on a hole (a birdie is a hole made in one shot below par). For a random sample of thirty-five male Professional Golfers' Association (PGA) players in 1997, Clark looked at their hole-specific scores for the tournaments they played in. He then calculated for each player the percent of time one birdie-or-better outcome was followed by another, and the percent of time that a par-or-worse outcome immediately preceded a birdie-or-better one (although each player generated data for multiple tournaments, Clark did not include the carryover sequence from the last hole of one tournament to the first hole of the next tournament). For the overall sample of golfers, the two percentages were an identical 19 percent; in other words, scoring a par or worse on one hole did not impair golfers' ability to achieve a birdie or better on the next hole, as this occurred just as often as a birdie or better on the previous hole being followed by a birdie or better on the next hole.[1]

In another study, Clark focused on full-round scores (relative to par) from golfers on the PGA, Seniors' (SPGA), and Ladies' (LPGA) tours, for each year from 1997 to 2000. Each player was analyzed separately. As Clark described the procedure, "Starting with the first tournament of the year for a player, Round 1 was compared with Round 2, Round 2 with Round 3 and, where applicable, Round 3 with Round 4. Moving to the next tournament for the same player in that year, Round 1 was compared to Round 2."[2] Readers with some statistical training may recognize this approach as that of a serial correlation. By correlation, we mean that if a player was hot (i.e., well below par) in one round, he would tend to be hot in the next round (or if cold in one round, cold in the next). Here is how Clark summarized his findings:

> For most years, evidence for round-to-round consistency was found for only a few players. For three of the four years on the PGA Tour (1997-1999) and LPGA Tour (1998-2000) and two of the four years on the SPGA Tour (1997 and 2000), the number of players showing round-to-round consistency exceeded chance expectations. However, this consistency in performance for individual players did not extend from one year to the next.[3]

If a player who exhibited streaky performance (i.e., consistency in hotness from one round to the next) in one year could repeat this accomplishment for additional years, it would provide evidence of someone being a streaky type of player. The lack of such repetition, however, suggests that players' streaky episodes may emerge substantially at random.

As has been noted in connection with other sports (i.e., the basketball study by Huizinga and Weil discussed in chapter 5, and the baseball study by Albright discussed in chapter 6), there are statistical techniques available for taking into account multiple factors, beyond simply success or failure on the previous attempt, that may affect success on the current attempt. Jeffrey Livingston conducted such a *multi-variate* study, using one tournament each from the PGA, LPGA, SPGA (now known as the Champions Tour), and Nationwide Tour (a men's tour just below PGA caliber) during 2006. Among the contextual factors studied were hole difficulty, based on "the average score on the hole by all players in all rounds," and a player's general ability level, based on his or her season-long average score per round.[4] Little or no evidence for streakiness was found for the PGA and SPGA/Champions players. Livingston's results for the other two tours were as follows:

> Nationwide Tour players show the most evidence of being subject to both the hot hand and the cold hand. . . . Female players on the LPGA Tour experience a weak hot hand effect. . . . However, they experience a potentially very strong cold hand effect. A long streak of bad holes makes it much less likely that a player will have a good hole on the next hole. Overall, while the magnitude of these effects is substantial, they are not large or robust enough to be considered the primary determinant of a player's success or failure.[5]

Cotton and Price, noting that previous streakiness studies have focused on highly experienced athletes, contend that "the hot hand, if it does exist, is likely driven by psychological factors including fluctuations in self-confidence, emotion and ability to remain focused, and that the impact these factors have on performance should decrease as individuals gain experience."[6] To test this idea, these researchers examined hole-by-hole statistical data from 12- to 17-year-olds participating in American Junior Golf Association tournaments. The main findings were that "the hot hand effect is most prevalent in the first year of tournament [play] with 13% of women and 4% of men [reaching the necessary statistical criterion, where 1% would be expected to meet the criterion simply by chance]. By the second and third year of tournament play the gender gap in the hot hand has disappeared with only about 2% of both men and women [meeting the criterion]."[7]

In conclusion, it appears that virtually any way you slice it (the body of data, not the ball off the tee), the evidence for streaky performance in actual rounds of competitive golf is very limited.

II
Extreme Hotness

8

Joe DiMaggio

New York Yankee Joe DiMaggio's major-league record 56-game hitting streak almost certainly has received a greater amount of statistical analysis than any other sports accomplishment. Set in 1941, DiMaggio's record streak is still being studied today. Widespread fascination with DiMaggio likely stems from many sources. On the field, his talent for streak hitting is unmatched. After DiMaggio finally went hitless in a game after getting at least one hit in each of the 56 straight games, he immediately got hits in his next 16 games, giving him a larger stretch of 72 out of 73 games with a hit.[1] Further, as a minor leaguer in 1933, DiMaggio had a hit streak of 61 games.[2] Off the field, DiMaggio not only played for baseball's most storied franchise, but he also had the celebrity aura of once being married to Marilyn Monroe. In this chapter, we'll review the various estimates that have been handed down over the years as to what the probability was of DiMaggio's 56-game hitting streak, given his overall batting abilities. As we'll see, there are analysts on both sides of the spectrum, some claiming extreme improbability—verging on miracle status—for DiMaggio's streak, but others contending that a spurt like DiMaggio's would fall well within the realm of established hitting abilities and random processes.

THE "EXTREME IMPROBABILITY" SCHOOL

Probably the best-known author to address DiMaggio's streak is the late Harvard paleontologist Stephen Jay Gould, who also wrote extensively about statistics in various contexts. Gould penned the following in 1988:

> My colleague Ed Purcell, Nobel laureate in physics but, for purposes of this subject, just another baseball fan, has done a comprehensive study of all baseball streak and slump records. His firm conclusion is easily and

swiftly summarized. Nothing ever happened in baseball above and beyond the frequency predicted by coin-tossing models. The longest runs of wins or losses are as long as they should be, and occur about as often as they ought to. . . .

But "treasure your exceptions," as the old motto goes. There is one major exception, and absolutely only one—one sequence so many standard deviations above the expected distribution that it should not have occurred at all. Joe DiMaggio's fifty-six-game hitting streak in 1941. . . . Purcell calculated that to make it likely (probability greater than 50 percent) that a run of even fifty games will occur once in the history of baseball up to now (and fifty-six is a lot more than fifty in this kind of league), baseball's rosters would have to include either four lifetime .400 batters or fifty-two lifetime .350 batters over careers of one thousand games. In actuality, only three men have lifetime batting averages in excess of .350, and no one is anywhere near .400 (Ty Cobb at .367, Rogers Hornsby at .358, and Shoeless Joe Jackson at .356). DiMaggio's streak is the most extraordinary thing that ever happened in American sports. . . . He beat the hardest taskmaster of all, a woman who makes Nolan Ryan's fastball look like a cantaloupe in slow motion—Lady Luck.[3]

Many other academic writers have also examined DiMaggio's streak. James Lackritz emphasized the distinction between plate appearances (all trips to the plate) and official at-bats (which exclude walks, hit-by-pitch, sacrifices, etc.). As long as a player has at least one official at-bat in a game, failure to get a hit in the game would end the streak. Walking (or other outcomes that make an at-bat unofficial) is thus harmful to maintaining a hitting streak, as it limits a player's opportunities to get a hit. An exception would be if *all* of a player's at-bats in a game were unofficial, in which case that game would be treated as neutral—neither extending nor ending the streak. Lackritz's main finding regarding the probability of a DiMaggio-like feat is as follows:

Even if a hitter could have [a batting average of] .448 leading to [a hits-per-plate-appearance rate of] .400 (in actuality, a value this high is unlikely), the chances of matching the 56-game streak is .00091 over any 56-game series and .012 for doing it at some point over the course of a full season.[4]

Though probabilities of roughly 1-in-1,000 (the .00091) and 1-in-100 (the .012) are hardly astronomical, the stipulated batting average in the example (.448) accentuates the improbability of a 56-game hitting streak.

From Different "Walks" of Life

Joe D'Aniello, one of the many authors to write on the DiMaggio hitting streak, included an interesting section in his article with the heading "What about Ted Williams?" The same season as DiMaggio's streak (1941), Williams batted .406, which is the last time any major-league hitter has recorded a batting average of .400 or above. Amazingly, even looking just at the portion of the season during which DiMaggio was hitting in 56 straight games, Williams compiled a higher batting average than did DiMaggio, .412 to .408. And yet, on lists of history's longest hitting streaks, Williams's name is nowhere to be found. The reason, according to D'Aniello, is that Williams had a "penchant for walking [that] made it virtually impossible for him to sustain a long hitting streak."[5] Drawing walks reduces a player's official at-bats, making it more likely he will get caught hitless in a game. In 1941, DiMaggio walked 76 times (21 times during the streak). Williams walked 147 times that season.

A similar phenomenon took place in the 2010 college baseball season, in which Florida International University's Garrett Wittels ended with an intact 56-game hitting streak.[6] One thing that helped Wittels was his low rate of getting walks: just 22 of them in his 56 games during 2010.[7] Wittels entered the 2011 season only two games short of the NCAA Division I hitting-streak record of 58 games, set in 1987 by Oklahoma State's Robin Ventura (who also had a long major-league career). However, on opening night of the 2011 season, Wittels went zero-for-four, ending his streak.[8]

Perhaps the most dismissive of any realistic chance of anyone equaling or exceeding DiMaggio's hitting streak are Providence College colleagues Bob Brown and Peter Goodrich.[9] They literally created one million simulated seasons of a player with DiMaggio's profile of batting statistics from 1936 to 1940. During this time, DiMaggio's hit-per-plate appearance rate was .314 (his batting average was .343) and he was making 4.5 plate appearances per game. With his "failure" rate per plate appearance at .686 (based on 1 minus his success rate of .314), taking $(.686)^{4.5}$ yields a probability of .183 for a "perfect run" of failure in a game (see chapter 2 for discussion of these formulas). Removing the probability of complete failure in a game (i.e., taking 1 minus .183), Brown and Goodrich thus arrived at a probability of .817 for DiMaggio getting at least one hit in a game. These authors then did the equivalent of flipping a coin with a .817 success probability 139 times (the number of games the "Yankee Clipper" played in 1941) to simulate a season. And they did this one million times. Brown and Goodrich found that, within these million seasons, hitting streaks of 56 games or longer occurred 222 times, a ratio of .000222, or about once every 5,000 seasons. Here's how they summarized the implications of their findings: "We are sure of this: what DiMaggio did in 1941 has no chance, realistic or otherwise, of ever happening again."[10]

THE "NOT SO IMPROBABLE" SCHOOL

During the spring of 2008, Samuel Arbesman, a graduate student at Cornell University, and Steve Strogatz, a professor at the Ivy League school, published a new set of hitting-streak computer simulations in an unlikely place—the op-ed page of the *New York Times*.[11] Like Brown and Goodrich, the Cornell team used a probability of .81 for DiMaggio's likelihood in 1941 of registering at least one hit in any given game. Arbesman and Strogatz did not, however, confine their examination just to the Yankee star or any particular year, noting that "the right question is not how likely it was for DiMaggio to have a 56-game hitting streak in 1941. The question is: How likely was it that anyone in the history of baseball would have achieved a streak that long or longer?"[12] Accordingly, a single version of their simulation involved "every player in the history of the game, for every season in which he played," which they described as "a simulation of the entire history of baseball."[13] Ultimately, baseball's entire history was simulated 10,000 times. The Cornell team's conclusion: "Streaks of 56 games or longer are not at all an unusual occurrence. Forty-two percent of the simulated baseball histories have a streak of DiMaggio's length or longer. You shouldn't be too surprised that someone, at some time in the history of the game, accomplished what DiMaggio did."[14] Perhaps the biggest surprise: "Joe DiMaggio is nowhere near the likeliest player to hold the record for longest hitting streak in baseball history."[15]

Perhaps a 42 percent chance of a DiMaggio-type streak sounds too high to you. It did to Iowa State University graduate student David Rockoff and Cal Poly–Pomona professor Phil Yates.[16] They noted that Arbesman and Strogatz had "treated a player's at-bats per game as constant across all games in a season."[17] It's easy to see why this would be a big issue. During a consecutive-games hitting streak, the bane of a batter's existence would be if he received only one or two official at-bats in a game, perhaps due to being walked multiple times. With so few official at-bats in a game, one obviously has little margin for error in keeping a hitting streak alive. By taking a player's average number of at-bats (or of plate appearances) for a season and using that for *all* games in a computer simulation, the analyst is (perhaps inadvertently) insulating a batter against a low-at-bat game.

Rockoff and Yates dealt with this issue by varying each player's at-bats randomly within a season (proportionate to how often the particular player actually would get 0, 1, 2, 3, 4, 5, etc., official at-bats during the season). With this adjustment, the probability of a DiMaggio-like streak dropped to 2.5 percent. This figure is small, but not so small (to me at least) that one cannot get his or her mind around it. Further, in getting actual player statistics to set up the simulation probabilities, Rockoff and Yates used a data source that was limited primarily to games from 1953 onward. Arbesman and Strogatz noted in their article that the most streak-conducive eras were the 1920s and 1930s and before. Thus, had Rockoff and Yates used the full historical record of baseball, they may well have come up with a higher estimate than 2.5 percent.

The most recent estimates I'm aware of come from Don Chance (isn't that a great name for a probability analyst?) and from Wayne Winston. Chance's 2009 article put the probability of a 56-game hitting streak at around 4 percent, with the author looking at the likelihood of a DiMaggio-type streak from the top 100 hitters in MLB history (players whose career averages ranged from .311 to .366).[18] He concluded that "if the entire history of baseball could be played 23 times, we would expect at least one 56-game hitting streak from these 100 players."[19] Winston estimated a 2 percent chance of at least one 56-game hitting streak from 1900 to 2006.[20]

If you've had enough of computer simulations and probabilities, there's a much simpler approach to studying hitting streaks that may change how you look at them. In asking how close various hitters have come to DiMaggio's streak, the typical answer has been to use what we might call a *deficit* model. In other words, if a player had a hitting streak snapped at thirty games, we would say he came up twenty-six games short of DiMaggio. To Trent McCotter, the University of North Carolina student, this type of answer did not do justice to how close some hitters actually had come to duplicating or exceeding DiMaggio's streak. In the *Baseball Research Journal*, McCotter pointed out that we can look not only at how many consecutive games a player hit in before going hitless in a game, but also how many straight games he hit in *after* the end of the previous streak. For example, if a player hit in 30 straight games, had one hitless game, then hit in the next 25 games, we could say the player was only *one* game short of a 56-game hitting streak. The only thing standing between the player and a tie with DiMaggio's streak would be the one-game hitless gap between the streaks of 30 and 25 games. We could thus call McCotter's approach the *gap* model. In McCotter's initial and follow-up articles, he identified several hitters in MLB history who came within one, two, or three hitless games of tying or exceeding DiMaggio's record.[21]

McCotter discovered that Bill Dahlen of the 1894 Chicago Colts (a forerunner of the Cubs) had compiled hitting streaks of 42 and 28 games, with only one hitless game in between. Under the gap model, therefore, Dahlen was one game short of a 71-game hitting streak (in fairness to DiMaggio, as noted at the beginning of this chapter, he was once only one hitless game short of a 73-game streak).

Among recent players:

- The Yankees' Derek Jeter was once two games shy of a 61-game hitting streak (25 straight games with a hit, 1 without, 14 with, 1 without, and 20 with, which I'll abbreviate as 25-X-14-X-20, spanning 2006–2007).
- Johnny Damon, playing for the Boston Red Sox in 2005, was three games short of a 57-game streak (29-X-5-X-15-X-5).
- The Seattle Mariners' Ichiro Suzuki came up three short of 56, in 2007 (25-X-X-19-X-9).

McCotter thus speculates that "it may just be a matter of time before [DiMaggio's streak] is seriously challenged…"[22]

CONCLUSION

On a purely mathematical basis, taking into account all the seasons of baseball that have been played (and will be played) and all the individual players involved, one could argue that a DiMaggio-like streak is at least within the realm of possibility. However, as Trent McCotter and other analysts have pointed out, there's an important factor that complicates the application of our mathematical formulas.[23] That factor is *awareness*, namely the knowledge on the part of fans, the media, and the player himself that he currently is on a long hitting streak and possibly closing in on records. Awareness can potentially help or hurt a batter's chances of prolonging the streak. On the positive side, a batter may intentionally give up the big home-run swing and be able to put balls into play for singles. On the negative side, media pressure and opposing pitchers who might want to walk batters on a hitting streak, would presumably work against perpetuation of the streak. Obviously, not all the answers are in—or else researchers wouldn't still be studying the DiMaggio streak 70 years after the fact!

He Messed with Texas

The Angels' Vladimir Guerrero once had a 44-game hitting streak, but you won't see it listed among the all-time MLB streaks of 40 games or longer. That's because Guerrero's streak occurred only in games against the Texas Rangers. The streak ended on August 5, 2006. According to an Associated Press article from the day before the spurt ended, Guerrero's *opponent-specific* streak was unprecedented in nearly 50 years (or perhaps longer): "Vladimir Guerrero went two-for-four to extend one of baseball's most peculiar streaks. He has hit safely in all 44 games he has played against Texas in his career, the longest stretch by any player against one team since 1957—which is as far as Stats Inc. has been able to research it."[24] Apparently, the Rangers finally got the message and acquired Guerrero themselves, prior to the 2010 season.[25]

9

Really Hot Teams

As Super Bowl XLII reached the final minutes of play on February 3, 2008 (marking the end of the 2007 season), the drama and excitement were immeasurably high. The New England Patriots had gone 16–0 in the regular season (beating the New York Giants in the finale), plus they had won two playoff games to reach the Super Bowl with an overall record of 18–0. The Pats' Super Bowl opponent was none other than the same Giant squad and, as in the regular season, New York was giving New England all it could handle. The Patriots finally broke through for a potential game-winning score with 2:45 left in the game, as Tom Brady hit Randy Moss for a 6-yard touchdown pass; the extra point made it 14–10 New England. Ultimately, of course, the Patriots' dream of an overall 19–0 season was not to be, as the Giants scored a touchdown of their own with 39 seconds remaining (aided on the drive by a miracle throw and catch).

It had been a long time since American sports fans (assuming they were old enough) had seen a streak like the Patriots'. One had to go back thirty-five years to find a comparable football streak, as the 1972 Miami Dolphins completed a perfect regular season (then fourteen games) and postseason to finish 17–0 (capped off in Super Bowl VII on January 14, 1973). For whatever reason, the early 1970s were a great time for team winning streaks. The 1971–1972 Los Angeles Lakers won a pro-sports record thirty-three straight games during the middle of the season (discussed at length in a later section). In the same city, Coach John Wooden's UCLA men's basketball team won eighty-eight straight games encompassing January 23, 1971 to January 17, 1974 (including postseason games, where the Bruins won three national championships within the streak).[1] Yes, there have been some major streaks during the decade of the 2000s—baseball's Oakland Athletics winning twenty consecutive games in 2002, and the University of Connecticut women's basketball team compiling separate winning streaks of 90 and 70 games—but they never seemed to capture as much public attention as did the earlier streaks. They nevertheless raise some interesting statistical issues, as will be discussed at length. Finally, as discussed in chapter 1, college football has also seen some lengthy streaks in the past decade—the Miami Hurricanes (2000–2002) and USC Trojans (2003–2005) each won 34 straight games—although these were well short of Oklahoma's record 47-game winning streak from 1953 to 1957.

In this chapter, I share my—and others'—estimates of the probabilities of some of these streaks. As discussed in earlier chapters, the starting point for estimating the probability of a streak is a player or team's prior base rate of success. For baseball hitting streaks, for example, we can use a player's batting average to derive a probability of his getting at least one hit in a game. When looking at team winning streaks, we have to look at a team's base rate of winning games. In the case of the UCLA men of the early '70s or the UConn women of the 2000s, where the winning streaks stretched over multiple seasons, one would be tempted—not unreasonably, in my view—to say that either of these teams, at its peak, had close to a 100 percent chance of winning each game. But, of course, no team literally has a 100 percent chance of winning a game. My solution to this dilemma is to make assumptions. What would be the probability of a team going on a winning streak of such-and-such length, if we assumed an underlying baseline probability of 95 percent, or 90 percent, or whatever, of the team winning in any particular game? Though these kinds of results must be taken tentatively, they can often help put things in perspective. If nothing else, they allow us the rhetorical device of saying that, *even if* we assume a very high underlying probability of a team winning in any given game (which should render a streak less impressive as, for example, the team may have enormously greater talent than its opponents), a streak of great length is *still* extremely unlikely.

LAKERS' 33-GAME WINNING STREAK

On January 9, 2007, the 35th anniversary date of the ending of the Lakers' 33-game winning streak, I conducted an analysis for my Hot Hand website in which I attempted to estimate the probability of the streak. At the time of the streak, I was nine years old, growing up in Los Angeles, so perhaps the Lakers' incredible stretch was one of the formative events in getting me interested in streaks.

In retrospect, it's hard to imagine that the 1971–1972 Lakers would dominate the NBA the way they did, with their 33-game winning streak, 69–13 regular-season ledger (an NBA record at the time), and relatively easy march through the playoffs (with no series closer than 4–2). The Lakers had lost the NBA finals in 1968, 1969, and 1970, and then were eliminated in the next year's Western Conference finals as the Milwaukee Bucks—a relatively new franchise, now featuring young star center Lew Alcindor (later Kareem Abdul-Jabbar)—romped to the 1971 NBA title. By the start of the 1971–1972 season, therefore, the Lakers probably would have struck most observers as an over-the-hill team. Although center Wilt Chamberlain (age 35 during the 1971–1972 season) and guard Jerry West (age 33) were still productive, years of knee injuries appeared to be catching up with veteran forward Elgin Baylor. The Lakers did have one newcomer who had the potential to breathe new life into the team—Coach Bill Sharman. According to Charley Rosen's book about the 1971–1972 Lakers, the team started out pretty well, but there was a feeling that Baylor was holding the squad back. Writes Rosen, "Baylor was selfish and defenseless. . . . There was only one thing for Sharman to do—arrange a retirement party for Baylor."[2] (I personally found the book useful for reminding me of key points in the streak, but according to a review at Amazon.com, the book appears to have quite a few factual errors in its details.)

In fact, it was immediately after Baylor's departure that the Lakers began their streak, beating Baltimore 110–106. Along the way, the Lakers surpassed the previous NBA record winning streak—20 games, set the year before by none other than Milwaukee—and the previous pro sport record of 26 straight wins by the 1916 New York (baseball) Giants. In addition to being the previous year's NBA champion and holding the previous NBA record winning streak, the ubiquitous Milwaukee Bucks had another place in the story, spanking the visiting Lakers 120–104 on January 9, 1972, to end L.A.'s victory streak at 33 games.

As we've seen in earlier chapters, to estimate the probability of a perfect sequential run, we multiply the probabilities of the individual components (wins). If there were a uniform probability of the Lakers' winning each game (the way a coin always has a .50 probability of being a head), we would raise that probability to the 33rd power. However, the 33 games in the streak would obviously have varied in their degree of difficulty, based on quality of opposition, home/road status, and perhaps other factors. To account for these considerations, I adopted a very simple model that pegged the difficulty of each game on whether the Lakers were at home or away and on the opponent's winning percentage from the previous season (the streak occurred early in the 1971–1972 season, so same-season record probably wouldn't have added much). Based on opposing teams' 1970–1971 winning percentages, I created four classes of difficulty. The Bucks' .805 percentage put them in a class by themselves, which I called Group A. Six teams' percentages clustered within .537–.634, so I called this Group B. Another five teams' percentages ranged from .439–.512, so they were Group C. Finally, three teams that were first-year expansion franchises that season—Buffalo (later the Los Angeles Clippers), Cleveland, and Portland—had winning percentages from .183 to .354, thus constituting Group D. The Lakers did not play the remaining team, Cincinnati (later Sacramento), during the streak. Then I assigned (assumed) Laker-winning probabilities to the thirty-three games based on the following rules:

D opponent at home for Lakers:	.90
D opponent on the road:	.85
C opponent at home:	.80
C on road or B at home:	.75
B opponent on road:	.70
A opponent at home:	.65
A opponent on road:	.60

I purposely tried to err in the direction of making these probabilities too high, so that the product of the 33 probabilities would not be overly small. For what it's worth, my estimate of the overall probability of the Lakers' winning all 33 of the games they did during the streak is .0002, or *1 in 5,000*. Consider the following:

- The NBA has been around for almost 65 years (founded in 1946).
- There are currently 30 NBA teams, and there have been at least 22 teams since the 1976–1977 season.
- Since the 1967–1968 season, each team has played 82 games per season, which creates a lot of theoretical opportunities for a team to start a 33-game winning streak.

Without doing any more math, it looks to me that over the entire history of the NBA, there would probably have been several thousand opportunities for such a streak. Thus, the Lakers' streak might not be that far out of line.

Contemporary observers would probably cite travel as a factor for why a team would be unlikely to win 33 straight games today. However, if you look at the 1971–1972 Lakers' game-by-game log,[3] you'll see that from December 17 to 22, they played five games in six nights (including three straight nights), which is not done anymore (according to an NBA webpage I found, "Teams cannot play three games on three consecutive nights").[4] Moreover, remember the Lakers' aging roster!

Another aspect to look at is the Lakers' margins of victory during the streak. They had one overtime game, December 10, against Phoenix. Other than that, the point differentials were distributed as follows:

- 9 games won by 4–9 points
- 15 games won by 10–19 points
- 5 games won by 20–29 points
- 3 games won by 30 or more

On the whole, the Lakers' victory margins were pretty healthy, so they may have been able to conserve energy by blowing away some teams early and resting the starters. Indeed, ESPN.com's Bill Simmons cites talent dilution—with the NBA adding several new teams in the late 1960s and early 1970s and the upstart American Basketball Association luring some top NBA players away—as producing many weak opponents for the Lakers to feast on.[5]

Finally, if you want to see an alternative statistical approach, I would recommend a piece by Gabe Farkas at *Courtside Times*. Although Farkas starts out discussing the super-streaky Laker squad, he ultimately uses the 1995–1996 season, in which the Chicago Bulls surpassed the 1971–1972 Lakers' 69–13 record by going 72–10, for his major analyses.[6]

PATRIOTS' QUEST FOR PERFECTION

Nearly a year after I had developed my little methodology for estimating the probability of the Lakers' 33-game winning streak, I decided to apply the same approach to estimating the probability of the 2007 Patriots' 16–0 season (posted on my website, December 30, 2007). After looking at the final win-loss records of New England's 13 unique opponents (the Pats played their three intra-divisional rivals twice), I grouped the opponents into five levels of difficulty:

- A (hardest opponents): The Patriots faced the Colts and Cowboys, each of whom won 13 games.
- B: Teams that won 10 or 11 games, comprising San Diego, Cleveland, Pittsburgh, and the New York Giants, formed the second-toughest tier of opponents.
- C: Teams that won from 7 to 9 games, comprising Buffalo, Cincinnati, Washington, and Philadelphia, were deemed to be "mediocre" opponents.

- D: Teams that won 4 or 5 games, specifically the New York Jets and Baltimore, were considered "weak" opponents. The Ravens actually gave the Patriots one of their biggest scares, but that's neither here nor there, given my system of basing opponents' strength on objective win-loss records.
- E: The Dolphins (1–15) were in a class by themselves, providing the Patriots with their easiest opposition.

For each combination of opponent strength and home/away status, I came up with the following (assumed) probabilities of the Patriots' winning any given game (the guidelines below are similar, but not identical, to those I developed for the Lakers).

E opponent at home for Patriots:	.95
E opponent on the road:	.90
D opponent at home:	.85
D opponent on the road:	.80
C opponent at home:	.75
C on road or B at home:	.70
B opponent on the road:	.65
A opponent at home:	.60
A opponent on the road:	.55

The 16 individual game-specific Patriot-win probabilities were then multiplied together, yielding .006; in other words, the chances of a perfect regular season like the Patriots' would be 6 out of 1,000 or roughly *1 in 167*.

In any given season, just at a *theoretical* level, one or two teams (at most) might be expected to contend for 16–0. One must take into account the head-to-head aspect (especially within a conference); having teams play each other directly rules out the possibility of both going 16–0. To take the match-up in Super Bowl XIX (after the 1984 regular season) as an example, the NFC champion San Francisco 49ers had gone 15–1 in the regular season and the AFC champion Miami Dolphins had gone 14–2, so having a pair of teams threaten to go 16–0 in the same season is not totally farfetched. Thus, if we held out the possibility of two teams per year *possibly* being able to go 16–0, then we would expect one team roughly every 85 years actually to do so (2 contenders per year x 85 years = 170, similar to the 1-in-167 figure I came up with, above). The 2007 NFL regular season was the 30th played under a 16-game format.

Not Just Unbeaten, But No Points Allowed!

During the 1939 college football regular season, the University of Tennessee squad took perfection to a new level. The Volunteers not only won all 10 of their games; they did not allow a single point along the way (Tennessee did lose to the University of Southern California in the Rose Bowl following the regular season, however, thus ending both the Vols' winning and shut-out streaks). According to the 2009 Tennessee football media guide (accessible via UTsports.com), "The 1939 team is the last team in NCAA history to be unscored upon in regular season play." Led by Coach R. R. Neyland (for whom the university's stadium was later named), Tennessee's defense had an amazing run that actually went beyond 1939. The 1938 Vol squad scored shut-out victories in its final five games of the season (including a bowl game), whereas the 1940 team blanked eight opponents. A good source to read more about these Tennessee teams is *The College Football Book*, produced by Sports Illustrated.[7] I first learned about this era in Volunteer football by randomly leafing through this volume in a bookstore.

OAKLAND ATHLETICS' 20-GAME WINNING STREAK

The 2002 Oakland Athletics' 20-game winning streak, which was one of the vignettes with which I began this book, was notable for several reasons. It became the new record in baseball's American League. It figured prominently in the book *Moneyball* about how A's General Manager Billy Beane, working with a much smaller budget than other top-caliber teams, made novel use of statistics to acquire players whose talents were underappreciated by other teams.[8] And, it was perhaps the first major streak to occur in the Internet Age, allowing statisticians (professional and amateur) to get a debate going about the odds of the A's streak, by blogging about it and e-mailing their calculations to baseball writers. As an example of the latter phenomenon, ESPN.com columnist Rob Neyer (who has also written several interesting baseball books) began writing about the 2002 A's streak in early 2003.[9] Before long, he was bombarded by e-mails offering different estimates of the probability of the streak, ranging from 1-in-955 to 1-in-500,000.[10]

I put in my two cents on my Hot Hand website with some computer simulations, the results of which matched roughly with some calculations I did

(I'm going to focus on the simulations I did, but the readers interested in the calculation formulas are encouraged to look at the writings of probability theorist William Feller,[11] not to be confused with Hall of Fame pitcher Bob Feller). Oakland's winning percentage for the entire 2002 season was .636 (103 wins and 59 losses), which I used as the team's "true value" for winning percentage (assuming the team's play can be simulated by a "generator" that yields wins with a .636 probability for each game). The season earlier, 2001, the A's won at a .630 clip, suggesting they really did have a stable true value at that point in their history. (As an aside, one of Neyer's correspondents sent in an estimate of 1-in-8,500 for the probability of the A's streak, which comes from taking .636 raised to the 20th power, although this formulation does not take into account the team's multiple opportunities over the course of a season to launch a streak.)

In order to simulate a 162-game season, I obtained a sequence of 162 random numbers, each from 1 to 100. In order to implement a 64 percent chance of a win in any given game (rounded from .636), I said that a randomly generated number from 1 to 64 would represent a win and one from 65 to 100, a loss. I didn't just examine one simulated season, of course; I examined 100 of them (as we've seen, statisticians have sometimes conducted thousands or even millions of iterations of a simulation; my simulations were fairly primitive, with a lot of visual inspection, so I contented myself with 100). The two pieces of data I needed to extract from each of the 100 simulated seasons were the total number of wins in the season and the longest winning streak within the season. I wanted to see how often a 20-game winning streak came up under the "chance" or "independence" conditions of the random-number generator.

Given that the actual 2002 A's won 103 games and the randomization device to generate wins and losses was tied to the team's actual winning percentage, it should come as no surprise that the most common outcome of the 100 simulated seasons was for Oakland to win 103 games (or thereabouts). However, there is also some random fluctuation involved, so that in some of the simulated seasons, the A's might win 99 games, or 107, or 112, etc. As an analogy, a coin has a true percentage of 50/50 heads and tails, yet the number of heads observed in sequences of 100 tosses would not always be exactly 50 and would show some variation. The first graph (figure 9.1) shows the distribution of how many times (out of the 100 simulations) a season with a given number of wins occurred.

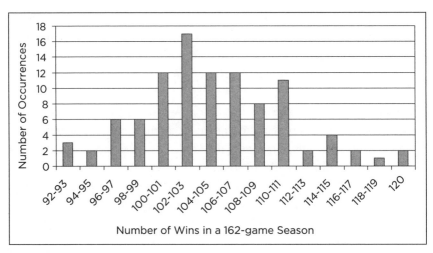

Figure 9.1

As can be seen, the most commonly occurring win totals (the mode) were 102 and 103 wins, corresponding closely to Oakland's actual performance (win totals were paired up into categories to simplify the chart). However, the (simulated) A's sometimes won as few as 92 or 93 games in a season, or as many as 120.

For each simulated season, I visually inspected the sequences of wins and losses and determined the longest winning streak. As shown in the next chart (figure 9.2), nearly one-fifth (19 out of 100) of the simulated seasons had 7

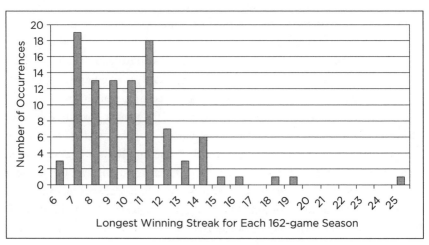

Figure 9.2

games as the length of their longest winning streak. Other common values for the length of a season's longest winning streak were 8, 9, 10, and 11; there were also several seasons in which the longest length of a winning streak was 12 or 14 games.

Other than one season where a 25-game winning streak emerged, in no season was there a winning streak longer than 19 games. In 6 of the 100 simulated seasons, a streak of 14 games emerged, but beyond that there was just a single season each with a streak of 15, 16, 18, 19, and 25 games. Clearly the A's, with their actual 20-game winning streak, were in rarefied territory. The average length of a "longest winning streak" over each of the 100 simulated seasons was 10.0 (it must be remembered that this distribution of seasonal longest streaks applies only for teams with a 64 percent chance of winning any given game; the distribution would be different for teams with different winning percentages).

The 25-game winning streak occurred in a season in which the simulated team won 111 games (well above what Oakland actually won in 2002). Naturally, the more games overall a team wins in a season, the greater its chance to produce a long winning streak. Since the real A's won 103 games the year of their streak, I think it's instructive to look at the longest winning streaks within each of the 7 simulated seasons that produced exactly 103 wins. The streak lengths are as follows:

7, 7, 8, 10, 10, 10, 13

Oakland's actual streak of 20 consecutive wins in a season in which the team won "only" 103 games thus appears to really stand out, relative to the longest streak lengths in the simulated seasons in which the A's also won 103 games.

Based on the chart of longest winning-streak lengths in the simulated seasons, the 20-game winning streak of the 2002 Oakland A's is something on the order of a once-in-a-hundred phenomenon (i.e., only one simulated streak equaled or exceeded 20 games). Considering that winning streaks of 18 and 19 games, as well, emerged in the simulations, it could perhaps be argued that a 20-game streak might occur about three times per 100 seasons. Note, however, that these projections hold only for a team with an underlying probability of winning 64 percent of its games (akin to the A's .636 winning percentage in 2002). If roughly one team per season plays at (or around) a .640 clip, then it might take anywhere from an estimated 33 to 100 seasons to see a 20-game winning streak. Of course, more than one team could play .640 ball or above in a single season, in which case we might expect to see Oakland's streak broken sooner than that. I did some research into the frequency of teams' winning 100 or more games per season in recent decades (100 wins correspond to a percentage of .617 out of the 162 games played by each team in a season; this is not exactly .640, but 100 is a nice round number of wins, which made it easier for me to search the Internet). In fact, recent decades of MLB play have seen an average of one team per season winning 100 or more games—a contributor on a Houston Astros' fan site counted 30 instances of a team reaching or exceeding the century mark in the 30 years from 1978 to 2007, although 14 of these instances have occurred in the 10 years from 1999 to 2008, an average of 1.4 teams per season.[12]

Defining the Question

The ubiquitous Jim Albert (along with his *Curve Ball* coauthor Jay Bennett) was kind enough to participate in an online "chat" in connection with my Hot Hand website, in October 2005. A year earlier, Albert had published an article on the Oakland A's 20-game winning streak. I also analyzed the A's streak, as shown in the main text of this chapter. The conclusion in Albert's article was as follows:

> Using a relatively simple, but realistic model for team competition . . . , we saw that long streaks of wins and losses are relatively common, and in fact 3.9% of the seasons in our simulation actually had a streak of length 20 or longer. . . . [Similar streaks would be expected] about 4% of the time, or about once every 25 years of baseball.[13]

My simulations suggested that streaks of 20 games or longer would be much more rare, especially if one took into account that Oakland's actual win total for the season, 103 games, would not be as conducive to a super-long streak as would a season with far more total wins. During the online chat, Albert thought my focus on the 103 wins to be inadvisable:

> I think the question, "What is a chance of a 20-game winning streak for a team with 103 wins?" is the wrong question. I think the right question is, "What is the chance that one team has a 20-game winning streak among all teams and many seasons?" I think the first question leads to a probability that is too small—we have introduced a bias since we are focusing on an interesting team. In contrast, in my paper, I showed that the second probability is relatively high.[14]

BASEBALL PENNANT-RACE COMEBACKS

Looking further back in baseball history, the most celebrated hot stretches would probably be those associated with teams' comebacks to rise from several games out of first place to winning a divisional or league pennant (prior to 1969, when East and West divisions were introduced, all National League [NL] teams competed in one set of standings for the league championship, as did all of the American League teams). A 2007 article summarized instances of teams coming back from deficits of double-digit games in the standings late in the season to finish in first place. These include the 1951 New York Giants who trailed the Brooklyn Dodgers by 13 games in August, and the 1978 New York Yankees who trailed the Boston Red Sox by 14 games in July. The Giants and Yankees each came back to win their respective league/divisional championships, in each case via a dramatic home run in a special playoff tie-breaker round (by the Giants' Bobby Thomson against the Dodgers, and the Yanks' Bucky Dent against the Red Sox).[15]

Another comeback worthy of this pantheon is the New York Mets' run to the 1969 NL East (and ultimately, World Series) title, overcoming the Chicago Cubs. The Mets, a 1962 expansion team created to restore a National League presence to the Big Apple after the Giants and Dodgers moved, respectively, to San Francisco and Los Angeles in 1958, had shown only futility leading up to 1969. The Cubs, meanwhile, reinforced their "lovable losers" image by what happened in 1969. In 2004, I analyzed the 1969 Mets-Cubs race on its 35th anniversary for my Hot Hand blog.

At the conclusion of play on August 31, the 1969 Chicago Cubs had a record of 83–52, putting them 4.5 games ahead of the New York Mets, who were 76–54. (The Cubs' game-by-game log lists a June 7 tie game, but I think it can be ignored.) Long-suffering Cub fans were eagerly anticipating their team's first return to postseason play since the 1945 World Series and perhaps first world championship since 1908. A torrid 11–1 Cub start to the 1969 season had hopes skyrocketing on the North Side of Chicago. The Mets' play through April and May of 1969 hardly suggested the emergence of an elite team, either, as the New Yorkers were 21–23 (.477). But, as shown in the two graphs in figure 9.3—month-specific winning percentages and cumulative winning percentages—the Mets started to get incredibly hot as the season moved along. New York's rise included a .679 month of June (19–9) and a .677 month of August (21–10). The Cubs, though unable to maintain their .696 pace of April, recorded separate monthly winning percentages of over .600 in each of May, June, and August (playing .517 ball in July).

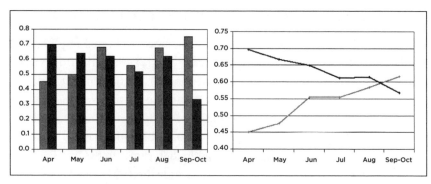

Figure 9.3   1969 Mets' (Gray) and Cubs' (Black) Winning Percentages, Each Month Alone (Left) and Cumulatively (Right)

Thus, the Cubs entered September with a 4.5-game lead over the Mets. For September and October combined (the regular season went only two days into October), the Mets followed up their awesome August with a sizzling September–October, closing the regular season at a .750 clip (24–8). The Cubs, meanwhile, went into free fall in September and October, playing at a .333 pace (9–18). When it was all said and done, the Mets (100–62, .617) won the division by eight games over the Cubs (92–70, .568).

Did the Cubs "choke" the last month of the season? I think most observers would answer affirmatively, though with an acknowledgement that the Mets' high winning percentage in the later months of the season certainly increased the difficulty of the Cubs' task. Given how hot the Mets got, the Cubs would have had to have gone 17–10 (.630) in September–October (i.e., giving them eight more wins than they actually achieved) in order to tie the Mets. But the Cubs had played at (or above) such a level for four of the first five months of the season. (The situation is actually a little more complicated than that. The Cubs and Mets played some games against each other, so each extra Cub win, when coming against the Mets, would have knocked New York down a win, making the Cubs' task easier. For simplicity, I ignore this element.) Various statistical questions can be asked—and answered:

What is the probability of a team (in this case the Cubs) with a cumulative .615 winning percentage over the first five months of the season (assumed to be a long-term base rate) winning nine or fewer of their final 27 games?

There was an estimated .003 probability that the Cubs would win nine or fewer games out of 27. Yet, that's what they did.

What is the probability of a team with a prior .615 winning percentage winning 17 or more out of 27 (what the Cubs needed to do)?

That would be .523. Thus, perhaps Cubs fans can console themselves with the realization that, given the Mets' hot play, chances were still only around 50/50 that the Cubs could play at a high enough level to stave off the Mets.

Looking at the Mets' side of the equation, what is the probability of a team with a .556 winning base rate (this was both the Mets' July-specific winning percentage and cumulative winning percentage through the end of July) winning 45 (or more) of 63 from August to October? (I know that I'm using different temporal cut-points for the Cubs and Mets, but the respective dividing lines appear to capture each team's "tipping point.")

That would be .007. Clearly, a lot of unlikely things had to happen for the Mets to overtake the Cubs in 1969.

Peter Golenbock's book *Wrigleyville* provides extensive interviews with players on the 1969 Cubs (see the chapter "Flying High in '69"). Much was made of the July 8 Cubs-Mets game in New York to open a three-game series, where Chicago outfielder Don Young made some crucial flubs to (apparently) cost the Cubs the game. As noted, however, the Cubs still led the Mets in the NL East standings by 4.5 games going into September. Interestingly, Golenbock quotes Cubs' second baseman Glenn Beckert as saying that the Mets "came from fifteen back," where in reality, as Golenbock notes, "they were 9 1/2 back at their worst."[16] Early in September, the Cubs suffered eight straight losses. Three games during that stretch really seemed to demoralize the Cubs, as the former players discussed in the book:

- September 7 at home at Wrigley Field against Pittsburgh. As Beckert recounts: "We had it locked. . . . And [the Pirates'] Willie Stargell hit a miracle home run."[17] Added Cub catcher Randy Hundley of the loss to Pittsburgh, "That, to me, was one of the toughest defeats we had the whole year, because that *really* busted our bubble. That was a tough defeat for us because we lost that game on Sunday, and the next day we went to New York to play the Mets. And that's when the Tommie Agee incident occurred, and losing that game *really* took some momentum out of our sails."[18]
- Indeed, on September 8, the Cubs lost 3–2 at New York. Agee, a Mets outfielder (now deceased), dominated this game by keeping his composure after a "knockdown pitch" and hitting a home run, then scoring a run later in the game on a controversial play at the plate.
- In Philadelphia on September 11, the Cubs tried a trick play in an attempt to pick off base runners, which backfired badly. Said Hundley, "To lose a game [4–3] that way was frustrating. Those kinds of things turn ball clubs around, and we could never get back on track, so that's why I said earlier,

the Don Young incident, as far as I was concerned, was irrelevant. Forget it. *This* was the period that knocked the wind out of our sails."[19]

Ultimately, however, a consensus developed among some of the players that the main reason for the Cubs' final-month collapse was fatigue, exacerbated by the team's policy at the time of playing only day games at home. Noted pitcher Fergie Jenkins, "The real reason was that we had played out the string. We were tired. Leo [Durocher, the manager] played the regulars almost the whole season. Billy [Williams] played 160 games, [Ron] Santo 160, Ernie [Banks] 150-some, [Don] Kessinger [157] and Beckert [129] played unless they were hurt, they played *all* the time. And Randy caught 150 games" (filling in of first or last names was done by me; Kessinger's and Beckert's numbers of games played appeared in brackets in the original text of the book).[20]

Unfortunately for Cubs fans, the frustrations have not ended. The team has made the playoffs a few times, but each time it looked like the Cubs would be heading to the World Series (such as in 1984 against San Diego and 2003 against Florida in the NL Championship Series), to borrow a cliché, the Cubs have "captured defeat from the jaws of victory." And, sometimes, the damage has even been self-inflicted.[21]

A Team That "Squashes" Its Opponents

ESPN.com ran an article in February 2009 about how a men's team at Connecticut's Trinity College had just completed its season with intact winning streaks of 202 consecutive matches and 11 national titles—in squash![22] As this book goes to press, Trinity still has not lost, winning the 2010 and 2011 national titles and extending its match-winning streak to 244.[23] According to the school's athletic website, this length constitutes "the longest winning streak in the history of intercollegiate varsity sports."[24] Trinity's national championships have come under the auspices of the College Squash Association rather than that of the NCAA (which oversees "big-time" sports such as basketball and baseball), but that shouldn't take away from Trinity's accomplishments—winning more than 200 straight matches at any level is pretty amazing.

UCONN WOMEN'S BASKETBALL

The University of Connecticut women's basketball program has made a habit, not only of winning NCAA national championships (seven of them), but doing so with perfect, undefeated seasons (four times). By compiling back-to-back 39–0 records in the 2008–2009 and 2009–2010 seasons[25] and winning their first 12 games of the 2010–2011 season, the Huskies achieved a 90-game winning streak (stopped by Stanford[26]), which broke the overall college basketball record of 88 straight by UCLA's men from 1971 to 1974. The recent 90-game streak was not the first time UConn had seriously threatened UCLA's mark. The previous time—and my first time conducting hot-hand analyses of the Huskies—came late in the 2002–2003 season when they lost 52–48 to Villanova in the Big East conference tournament final, ending what was then the NCAA Division I women's record of 70 consecutive wins, held by UConn.[27] The Huskies' stretch of 70 straight wins—never mind the 90 straight wins that came later—was a lot longer than the previous record streak in women's basketball, held by Louisiana Tech with 54 wins in a row from 1980 to 1982.

Stanford the Stopper

Women's basketball was not the only sport in which Stanford snapped another school's massive record-winning streak during 2010. On the volleyball court, the Stanford women put a halt to Penn State's 109-match run of victories.[28] To appreciate Penn State's dominance during its streak, keep in mind that a team must win three games (also known as sets) to win a match. Despite playing in the tough Big 10 conference and playing many difficult nonconference opponents as well, 101 of the Nittany Lions' wins were via 3-0 sweeps, and opponents took Penn State to a decisive fifth game (i.e., in which the teams were tied two games apiece) only three times.

Around the time UConn had reached 70 straight wins in 2003, I had been thinking about some type of statistical analysis to do in anticipation of the Huskies approaching the aforementioned UCLA record of 88. One kind of simple analysis I came up with involved the probability of UConn winning its next [fill in the blank] games, assuming the Huskies' probability of winning each individual game was something outlandishly high, such as .90, .95, or .99 (whereas UConn's probability of winning *some* of its games might have been that high, the Huskies' *a priori* win probabilities against top opponents such as Tennessee and Duke were obviously much lower). Such assumptions, as noted earlier, mainly help to put things in perspective and allow fans to marvel at the small likelihood of a phenomenal streak, even among great teams.

Having reached 70 straight wins, UConn needed another 18 to equal UCLA. Assuming a uniform .90 per-game win probability for UConn over an 18-game span, we would take $(.90)^{18}$. This yields a probability of only .15 that UConn could sweep 18 games, even with a per-game win probability of .90. If we raise the per-game win probability to .95 and look at $(.95)^{18}$ we only get about .40 for the probability of UConn sweeping 18 games, and if we raise the per-game probability to the extreme level of .99, then $(.99)^{18}$ would give UConn a probability of .83 of winning 18 straight. Another possible calculation, which really captured the momentous nature of the Huskies' 70-game streak, in my view, was to take $(.90)^{70}$. Even with the very optimistic .90 per-game winning percentage, Connecticut would have had only a .0006 probability of winning 70 straight. With UConn now establishing the new standard of 90 games for a college-basketball winning streak, the assumption of a .90 probability of winning each game yields an overall probability of .00008— less than 1-in-10,000—for the streak, $(.90)^{90}$.

A large contributor to Villanova's 2003 streak-shattering win over the Huskies, noteworthy in its own right for streakiness, was a 15–0 run in the second half, erasing a nine-point Connecticut lead. Interestingly, UCLA's 88-game streak was also ended by a big run, with Notre Dame scoring the final 12 points of the game to defeat the Bruins 71–70 (and that's well before the three-point shot was introduced to college basketball).

Is Perfection Truly Possible?

When the UConn women's hoop squad finished its 2009 season at 39–0, the Final Four that year was played in St. Louis. Among the journalists covering the event, therefore, was *St. Louis Post-Dispatch* sportswriter Tom Timmermann. Much of this book is about statistical oddities, so it's worthwhile to note that Tom and I knew each other as college sports-writers for the UCLA *Daily Bruin* in the early 1980s. Tom contacted me about the UConn streak heading into the championship game and was kind enough to cite my Hot Hand website in his article. Tom's article was largely philosophical, posing the question of whether a "perfect" season was truly possible, even if a team won all its games.[29] After all, a team's effort might not have been maximal at all times or it could have committed a large number of turnovers in a game, albeit still winning.

CONCLUDING THOUGHTS ON TEAM STREAKS

Not that theorizing about and performing calculations for individual-sport streaks (e.g., golf, tennis) are easy, but I find that doing the same for team-sport streaks raises the complexity to a new level! In the simplest case of an individual sport, we have to focus only on our focal player and his or her opponent, each of whom is likely to perform within a range of personal proficiency. In match-play bowling, for example, competitor A might have a seasonal average of 225, with two-thirds of his/her performances falling within 200–250, whereas competitor B might be averaging 215, with his/her own characteristic range. With this information, we can get an idea of how likely A would be to prevail over B in a given match, which allows us to estimate the probability of a given winning streak.

With team sports, of course, there are multiple athletes competing for each squad, each of whom may be performing toward the top or toward the bottom of his/her respective range of abilities. Take one of those classic 1980s NBA-championship series between the Boston Celtics and L.A. Lakers, for example. For Boston, Larry Bird might have been having a bit of an off-night in a particular game (which would still leave him performing at a pretty high level), but Kevin McHale and Dennis Johnson were at the top of their games, and Robert Parish was having an average night. For L.A., maybe Earvin ("Magic") Johnson was firing on all cylinders, but Kareem Abdul-Jabbar and James Worthy were a little down. How could an analyst possibly hope to integrate all this information?

Adding further complexity, team sports differ widely amongst themselves in how athletes' talents can be deployed. As Albert and Bennett noted in their 2005 online chat with the Hot Hand website, baseball greatly limits the use of teams' top players—a starting pitcher to once every four or five days, a great hitter to one out of every nine of a team's at-bats. In basketball, the Lakers and Cleveland Cavaliers (make that Miami Heat), respectively, can try to have Kobe Bryant and LeBron James take as many of the team's shots as possible. Sometimes, it's not the strongest, but the weakest, team member that's of greatest focus (recall the expression, "A chain is only as strong as its weakest link").

Back in the early 1970s, social psychologist Ivan Steiner developed a classification of group tasks (not specifically for sports, but also for workplace groups) that might help restore order to the complexity of team sports. The example where one player (a Bryant or James) can account substantially for a team's output is known as a *disjunctive* task. A "weakest link" situation, for example a track or swimming relay team where one slow member can cost the team precious time, is a *conjunctive* task.[30] Another type, an *additive* task, might apply to Davis Cup tennis. Each competition pits one country against another. In each of the four singles matches (which are played along with a doubles match), a player can contribute a team-point to his nation by beating his opponent. The first nation to (additively) achieve three team-points wins the contest. The question then becomes, is one type of task structure (in combination with a given team's distribution of talent) particularly conducive to winning or losing streaks? A team with good depth would seem likely to do well on additive tasks; in order to lose, more than one of the team's talented performers would have to play badly to cost the team a victory. In contrast, a team with one star, but little depth, might be able to get by in a disjunctive situation (Larry Bird's college team, Indiana State, which went 33–0 en route to making the 1979 national championship game before losing to Magic Johnson's more balanced Michigan State squad, comes to mind), but would be vulnerable to the star player having an off-night or being contained by the opposition. These examples merely scratch the surface of how task structure and team dynamics might affect streakiness. Now, when you see a team going on a long winning or losing streak, perhaps you'll start thinking about how the concepts of disjunctive, conjunctive, and additive tasks might apply.

I have not, of course, covered every notable hot streak in the history of team sports. I may perhaps have even missed one involving your favorite team. To supplement the text, I've included a table that provides other experts' rankings of top team streaks.

Ratings of Top Team-Sport Streaks

	ESPN.com (2001)	Allen St. John* *Made to Be Broken* (2006)
Lakers' 33-game NBA winning streak (1971–1972)	1	37
UCLA men's basketball seven straight NCAA titles (1967–73)	2	5 (for 88-game winning streak)
Oklahoma football 47-game winning streak (1953–1957)	3	46
Yankees' 11 straight MLB playoff series wins (1998–2001)	4	–
Celtics' eight straight NBA titles (1959–1966)	5	–
New York Giants' 26-game MLB unbeaten streak (1916)	6	–
Penguins 17-game NHL winning streak (1993)	7	–
Prairie View football 80-game *losing* streak (1989–1998)	8	–
North Carolina women's soccer 103-game unbeaten streak (1986–1990)	9	–
U.S. winning 13 straight Ryder Cups (men's golf; 1959–1985)	10	–
Yankees' five straight World Series titles (1949–1953)	HM	–
Montreal Canadiens' five straight Stanley Cups (1956–1960)	HM	–
Flyers' 35-game NHL unbeaten streak (1979–1980)	HM	–
Winnipeg Jets' 30-game NHL *winless* streak (1980)	HM	–
Penn State football 46 straight years without a losing season (1939–87)	HM	–
Canton Bulldogs' 25-game NFL unbeaten streak (1921–23)	HM	–
U.S. Olympic men's basketball seven gold medals in a row (1936–1968)	HM	–
1972 Miami Dolphins' perfect season	–	10

*St. John's book lists sports accomplishments, including streaks and other records (e.g., career number of home runs). HM = Honorable Mention

10

Hot Basketball Shooting

Joe DiMaggio, the 1971–72 Los Angeles Lakers, and the other teams discussed thus far are certainly not the only sports figures to record amazing hot streaks. The present chapter discusses several others in basketball, in more concise fashion.

FREE THROWS

Few basketball fans have not been exasperated by their favorite team's failure to make key free throws in an important game—or relieved to see the opposing team have a meltdown at the charity stripe. Memphis (2008), Kansas (2003), and Houston (1983) are but three teams who had the NCAA college basketball national championship in their grasp, only to lose it due to free-throw shortcomings. Yet, there have also been teams that distinguished themselves with uncannily "hot" free-throw shooting.

A March 2009 *New York Times* article pointed out that, averaging across large numbers of players, free-throw success rates have hit a ceiling over the past half-century:

> Since the mid-1960s, college men's players have made about 69 percent of free throws, the unguarded 15-foot, 1-point shot awarded after a foul. In 1965, the rate was 69 percent. This season, as teams scramble for bids to the N.C.A.A. tournament, it was 68.8. It has dropped as low as 67.1 but never topped 70.[1]

In the NBA, the figure has been around 75 percent, ranging from 71 to 77 percent.[2] In this context, therefore, it is particularly impressive that a select few teams in recent years have been able to maintain near-100 percent accuracy from the free-throw line for long stretches.

One such team was Wake Forest University in 2005. Entering their January 15 game against North Carolina with a .659 free-throw percentage, the Demon Deacons as a team went 32-of-32 from the line.[3] I remember watching the latter part of that game on television and, while writing this section of the book years later, I rechecked the box score and play-by-play sheet to refresh my memory. Just as I recalled, it was left to one of the team's big men, 6-foot-9 Vytas Danelius, who was not that great of a free-throw shooter (.686 in 2005), to hit the final pair, which he did. In the Deacons' next game (against Florida State), they made their first 18 free-throw attempts, which on top of the 32 straight from the previous game brought Wake's active streak to 50 consecutive successful free throws. However, the Florida State game was not over and, as it turned out, Wake Forest still had some work to do at the free-throw line. With the score tied and four seconds remaining, the Deacons had a free-throw attempt to possibly win the game—and missed.[4] The 50 straight free throws made by Wake Forest set a new NCAA record and got statistical analysts working on estimates of the probability of the streak. As we know, the most basic calculation would be to raise the team's prior success rate (.659) to the 50th power, yielding .0000000009 or about one in a billion. Ken Pomeroy, whose quote about Wake Forest we saw in chapter 2, analyzed the streak using not the team's overall free-throw shooting percentage, but rather each player's percentage, taking into account how many of the 50 shots he took. Noting that "the bad free throw

---

"Gym Rat" Free-Throw Specialists

Virtually all the streaks written about in this book pertain to actual game competition. However, there are some people who specialize in an athletic task and give exhibitions to showcase their skills. Free-throw shooting has a number of practitioners of this type. There's Dr. Tom Amberry, who according to his website (http://www.freethrow.com), once made 2,750 free throws with no misses in one day. There's also Ted St. Martin, who according to his website (http://www.sharpshooterfreethrows.com) holds the record of 5,221 consecutive-made free throws. Both of these gentlemen have been mentioned in the *Guinness Book of World Records*. Rick Rosser (http://focusfreethrows.spaces.live.com), who is featured in a YouTube video hitting a perfect 72-of-72 free throws in two minutes, once e-mailed me after seeing the Hot Hand website. I thank him for bringing my attention to this form of free-throw competition.

shooters . . . didn't participate much in this streak," Pomeroy came up with a less-astronomical streak probability, closer to 1 in 1.5 million.[5]

About a year and a half earlier, an NBA team did something similar. In Game 1 of the Western Conference final series between Dallas and San Antonio, the Mavericks made 49 straight free throws after missing their first one, thus going 49-of-50 as a team.[6] That year Dallas was an excellent free-throw shooting team, hitting .829 during the regular season. Because the Mavs generally shot well from the stripe, calculations showed their probability of making 49 (or more) free throws out of 50 to be almost exactly a 1-in-1,000 phenomenon. That's not as astronomical as Wake Forest's streak of a similar length, but impressive nonetheless.

TWO-POINT BASKETS

Major upsets are the "bread and butter" of the NCAA basketball tournament's popularity. From North Carolina State's buzzer-beating dunk off of a desperate long-distance shot in 1983 to stun Houston in the championship game, to 2005's first-round shocker by Bucknell over Kansas, upsets capture our imagination (except, perhaps, for fans of the losing school). Each upset has its own texture and storyline. For hot shooting by a team, the game that would probably first come to mind—provided one is old enough to have seen the game— is Villanova's upset win in the 1985 NCAA title game over Georgetown, by the score of 66–64. As noted in an ESPN Sports Century retrospective, "Defending national champion Georgetown, top-ranked in the country, is favored by 9½ points to defeat No. 8–seeded Villanova in the NCAA final. The first two games [the teams met in Big East conference play], though, were tight, with Georgetown winning 52–50 in overtime and 57–50."[7]

Georgetown was known for its tenacious defense, with future NBA star Patrick Ewing a dominant presence at center. As the ESPN retrospective also noted, Georgetown had held its opposition to a paltry 39 percent field-goal percentage. Yet, Villanova shocked the college basketball world with record-high shooting. Villanova made 22 of 28 field-goal attempts, for an incredible .786 percentage. This includes .90 shooting in the second half (9 of 10). The shot clock had not yet been introduced to NCAA tournament play, nor had the three-point shot. Thus, teams could assiduously work for good shots and not necessarily be rewarded for hitting from long-distance.

Not only was Villanova's shooting percentage against Georgetown an NCAA men's championship-game record, but the Wildcats really distanced themselves from many other great teams in championship-game history. As part of a 20-year retrospective on Villanova's torrid shooting night that I undertook in 2005 for my Hot Hand website, I compiled all team shooting percentages from NCAA men's title games from 1939 (the year of the first tournament) to 2004. A total of 66 title games had been played during those years, yielding a potential 132 team shooting percentage figures (i.e. 66 x 2 teams per game). A website called Hickok Sports (http://www.hickoksports.com) has compiled results and box scores from all NCAA men's basketball tournaments (and other athletic competitions). Apparently, for most of the early years, shooting percentage data are not available (for example, the box score of the 1939 title game appears to contain information on made field goals, but not attempts). I thus ended up with 112 team field-goal-percentage observations. Figure 10.1 shows a frequency plot (histogram), with shooting percentages (grouped into intervals) along the horizontal axis and the number of teams achieving a given shooting level depicted on the vertical axis. A "normal" (bell-shaped) curve is superimposed for comparison to the actual data. Villanova stands out on the far right of the diagram.

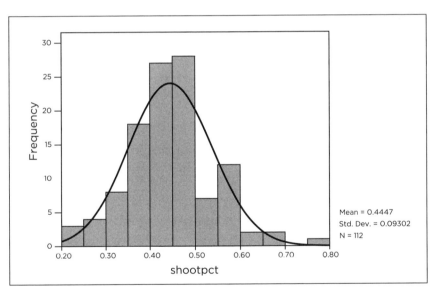

Mean = 0.4447
Std. Dev. = 0.09302
N = 112

Figure 10.1

A common metric for evaluating the location of a particular data point in relation to the full distribution is a z (or standardized) score (the score of the one data point minus the mean, all divided by the standard deviation; the SD represents the degree of spread in the distribution). Villanova's z score came out to about 3.7. Such a score suggests that Villanova's field-goal shooting percentage would be in the top fraction of the top 1 percent. There were relatively few actual observations, however, so our evaluation would appear to be more of an *inference* about Villanova's shooting in a hypothetical large, bell-shaped population distribution. Also, because field-goal shooting was not so good in the early years of the tournament (several teams shooting in the .20 and .30 vicinity), I redid the analysis excluding games prior to 1965 (the first year both teams exceeded .50). Removing low values would, of course, raise the mean, which I expected to diminish Villanova's z score. That did not happen. In retrospect, I realized that removing low scores also shrinks the standard deviation (i.e., how spread out the teams are), contributing to a larger z.

One might also have expected the advent of the three-point shot (beginning with the '87 tournament) to affect overall shooting percentages, as the longer-distance shots would presumably lower teams' hit rates. This may be true in the long run, but the three-point shot has not prevented some excellent shooting nights, such as those by Kansas (.64) in the '88 final, UNLV (.61) in the '90 final, Duke (.56) in the '91 final, and Michigan State (.56) in the 2000 final. Regardless of the statistical complexities, *suffice it to say that Villanova's shooting against Georgetown really stood out.* Perhaps the most amazing thing of all is how, with its great shooting, Villanova ended up winning by only two points!

Big Men Who Came Up Big

Along with stunning upsets, another element that gives March its "madness" during NCAA tournament play is the star player rising to the occasion when the pressure is on. Two prominent examples, each featuring a player who stood 6-foot-11, are Christian Laettner's game for Duke against Kentucky in the 1992 East Regional final and Bill Walton's for UCLA against Memphis State (now known as just Memphis) in the 1973 national championship game.[8] Laettner will, of course, best be remembered for his buzzer-beating turnaround jumper, after receiving a near length-of-the-court pass, to give Duke a 104–103 victory in overtime. What's probably not as well remembered is that Laettner had a perfect day shooting the ball against Kentucky. Quoting from the "Vault," *Sports Illustrated's* online historical repository, "Laettner doesn't miss. He's perfect. Twenty times on this night he took aim for the rim— 10 shots from the floor, 10 from the free throw line—and 20 times he scored. Perfect."[9] Walton wasn't perfect, but he was darn close. The big redhead hit on 21 of 22 shots from the field, in the Bruins' 87–66 win.[10]

THREE-POINTERS

Early in the 2006–07 men's college basketball season (around late November), the Texas Tech Red Raiders were leading the nation in three-point shooting percentage. Texas Tech had made 58 of 115 attempts from beyond the arc (50.4 percent). Among individual players nationally (excluding those who had only a couple of attempts), the leader at the same point in the season was BYU's Austin Ainge, who hit 12-of-17 (70.6 percent) treys (for those who are wondering, Austin is indeed the son of former NBA guard Danny). As I argued at the time on my Hot Hand blog, neither Texas Tech's 50 percent success rate as a team, nor Ainge's 70 percent rate, was likely to hold up for the entire season. The previous year's three-point percentage leaders at the end of the season were Southern Utah (team) at 42.9 percent and Northern Arizona's Stephen Sir (individual) at 48.9 percent, both well below the pace that Texas Tech and Austin Ainge were setting.

What we were likely seeing, I argued, was the extremity of results associated with small numbers of observations. This concept was first brought to my attention by Geoff Fong in the spring of 1984, when he was on the faculty at Northwestern and I was visiting during my tour of prospective graduate schools (I ultimately chose Michigan). Geoff was telling me about his research on statistical reasoning, and he pointed out how, early in every MLB season, the list of batting leaders will tend to have several players hitting above .400, yet there would be virtually no chance of any player ending the season at that level (the last player to hit .400 or better for a season was, of course, Ted Williams in 1941). Mark Hartwig describes the small-numbers phenomenon a bit more technically:

> All other things being equal, variation is more pronounced with small samples than with large ones. The larger your sample, the more stable your results will be. They will be less subject to the possibility that another study would produce greatly different results. A corollary is that large samples are less likely to produce extreme results. For example, assuming that you have a fair coin, it's much more difficult to get all heads when you toss a coin 50 times than when you toss it only two or three times.[11]

For illustrative purposes, I suggested using the 2005–2006 Texas Tech three-point success rate of .390 as a baseline estimate for the 2006–2007 squad. Though there had been some change in personnel, most of the Red Raiders' outside shooters from 2005 to 2006 were still on the team, including offensive stalwart Jarrius (Jay) Jackson. Using a statistical approach discussed in chapter

2, we could ask how likely it is that a .390 three-point shooting team (which is what the 2006–2007 Red Raiders were assumed to be, based on their statistics from the previous year) would make 58 (or more) treys in 115 attempts (which is what Texas Tech actually had done at the time it was leading the nation in three-point percentage). The answer is .008, a little less than 1-in-100, so what the Red Raiders were doing was already very rare statistically.

As noted, the larger the sample, the less susceptibility to unusually high or low success rates. To approximate a full season's worth of shots instead of just a quarter-season, I multiplied by four Texas Tech's current number of made threes (58 × 4 = 232) and number of attempts (115 × 4 = 460). The ratio of 232/460 is the same as the Raiders' late-November three-point percentage of 50.4, but would be a much longer-term accomplishment. Again, using .390 as a baseline, the team's probability of hitting 50.4 percent of 460 three-point attempts was much tinier than before, .0000004, about 4-in-10 million.

Another potentially relevant concept that I'd like to mention briefly is regression toward the mean. Regression toward the mean simply refers to the tendency for extreme values in the early rounds of performance—either extremely high or extremely low—to be followed by values more in the center of the distribution. Regression would also tend to bring Texas Tech's high three-point shooting percentage back toward a more typical level.

In the end, the Red Raiders indeed finished the 2006–2007 season with a .412 three-point shooting percentage (down from .504) and Austin Ainge finished the year with a .479 percentage on threes (down from .706). Texas Tech's decline in *absolute* three-point shooting percentage did not necessarily imply that the Red Raiders would drop from their late-November ranking of number-one in the nation, as other top teams would likely show declines in their three-point hit rates as well. For the record, however, Bradley ended up being the national team leader in three-point shooting percentage at .427, with Texas Tech dropping to ninth. As for the final individual statistics, Texas A&M's Josh Carter ended up leading the nation in shooting percentage from behind the arc at .516.

No sooner had I written on my blog about how extreme patterns most readily occur when looking at small numbers of observations and how it's hard to maintain extremely high (or low) levels of performance over larger numbers of attempts, than a Division III men's college basketball player did as much as can be done within a single game to contradict my assertions (basketball powerhouses such as UCLA, Duke, and Villanova play at the NCAA Division I level, with Division III featuring much smaller schools).

What happened to contradict my thinking was that Lincoln University's Sami Wylie shot 51 percent on three-pointers. If a player were to have shot (roughly) 50 percent on 10 three-point attempts, I would find that moderately interesting. In 20 attempts? More impressive; and so on as the number of shots from behind the arc increased. Well, in Wylie's case, he shot 51 percent on *41* attempts from three-point land. Yes, he shot 41 times from downtown, making 21 treys! In total, he ended up with 69 points in Lincoln's 201–78 win over Ohio State–Marion.[12] An ESPN.com article likened the game to a scene from the movie *Pleasantville*, where "every shot from every conceivable angle goes in."[13]

Whether or not the hot shooting streaks we've been discussing represent anything other than chance variation—such as a coin that's flipped 1,000 times coming up heads several times in a row—there's no question players *feel* like they're in a magical mental state. Known as the Zone, the state has been described as one of heightened concentration, relaxation, and absorption. Inspired by a January 26, 2007, game in which the New York Knicks' Jamal Crawford "hit 16 straight shots—the longest NBA streak in 10 years—including 8 from three-point distance," *Cigar Aficionado* writer Ken Shouler decided to investigate the Zone. Shouler quoted a variety of players and psychologists who thought there was something to it.[14] I was among the skeptics Shouler interviewed. I argued that for a "make-or-break" shot a team should try to get the ball in the hands of the player with the highest long-term shooting percentage, regardless or whether he or she appears to be in the Zone in any particular game. As I asked rhetorically during my interview with Shouler, "If Michael Jordan [had] hit only two of 12 shots on a certain night, does that mean that you want one of his teammates taking the last shot?"[15]

Two other players who have likely felt they were in the Zone are Derek Fisher, who has played most of his NBA career with the L.A. Lakers, and Jason McElwain, a Rochester, New York, high school student with autism. In 2002, as part of an exchange on a sports discussion website, one of the participants pointed out that Fisher had hit 75 percent of his three-point attempts (15-for-20) in a 2001 playoff series against San Antonio.[16] Perhaps rhetorically, the person on the discussion board asked of Fisher, "was he within his standard range or was he on a hot streak?" I immediately decided to run some simulations on Fisher, as well as research his actual regular-season and playoff three-point shooting percentages in the immediately preceding years. As I like to note periodically, a word of caution is in order whenever a player is chosen for analysis *specifically* based on having a reputation for streaky performance. The

DOES SUCCESS PLAY WITH OUR MINDS?

Players who are supposedly in the Zone often claim to perceive the physical equipment of their sport as being unusually friendly to them. A hot-shooting basketball player, for example, may say that the rim looked as big as a Hula-Hoop, or a hitter may claim to have seen the baseball as being much bigger than it actually is and with amazing visual clarity.

Purdue University's Jessica Witt and colleagues have conducted several studies over the years documenting that, indeed, successful athletes judge the sizes of their relevant sports objects as being larger than do their less successful competitors. In one study, softball players were shown circles of different diameters and were asked to guess which one was the same size as a softball. The better the hitter, the bigger was the estimate. Another study found the same type of results for golfers' estimates of the size of the hole. Finally, Witt studied football field-goal kickers and their judgments of the distance between the two upright poles the ball would have to go through. Similar to the earlier findings, the better kickers estimated having more space in which to place a successful field goal than did the less successful kickers.[17]

These studies appear to have a "chicken-and-egg" problem, however. Did the distorted size perception come first, affecting the player's confidence, or did the good (or bad) performance come first, thus affecting the player's mental image of the objects in question? In the football study, the researchers had the athletes estimate the size of the goalposts both before and after kicking. Size-distorted perceptions occurred only *after* the kicking, suggesting that success leads to the belief that the equipment was conducive to good performance.

potential is that, even if Fisher were found to be a true streak shooter, it could be argued that we were just sampling or "cherry picking" from a small, extreme segment of players, without any idea of how common similar streak-shooting performances might be among a representative cross-section of all players.

To cut to the chase, I am prepared to state that Derek Fisher was a bona fide, hot, streaky shooter, beyond chance, *in the 2001 NBA postseason*. I focused on his 2001 postseason as a whole (in which he was 35 for 68 from three-point range for a percentage of .515), because using just the four-game San Antonio series (in which Fisher shot the amazing .75) would probably be considered too short of an observation period by most statisticians. I used .40 as Fisher's "typical" three-point shooting percentage, as this roughly represents his regular-season performances in 2000–2001 (.397) and 2001–2002 (.413).[18] In a similar fashion to other computer simulations I have conducted and reported in this book, I requested 68 numbers from a random generator, each within the range of 1 to 100, to represent the 68 three-point shots Fisher took in the 2001 postseason. Because his base rate three-point shooting percentage was set at .40, a random number between 1 and 40 was considered a hit, and one from 41 to 100 a miss. I conducted this simulation 20 times. A fair coin that has a known 50-50 probability of a head or tail on each toss can nevertheless generate sequences of several heads (or tails) in a row simply by chance, so that the observed proportion of heads (or tails) in a given sequence can be something other than .50. For our purposes, we want to know how often an event-generator with a known .40 probability on each shot would generate a 68-shot sequence with a hit rate of .515 (what Fisher actually achieved), thus demonstrating chance variation.

In my 20 simulations, a .515 hit rate was *never* achieved. In other words, Fisher's actual 2001 postseason three-point shooting percentage of .515 could not be duplicated by chance variation from a .40 baseline, within 20 stagings of simulated postseasons. As those of you who have taken a college statistics course are probably aware, researchers typically refer to a result as being "statistically significant" if it would come up by pure chance 1 time out of 20 or less often ($p < .05$). In this sense, Fisher's actual performance was statistically significant, albeit based on a relatively small number of simulations. The simulation sequences with the highest hit rates made it up to .46 and .47. Not surprisingly, considering that the base rate was set at .40, 10 of the sequences had hit rates between .37 and .43. One went as low as .28. These results show that—for this particular exercise at least—*observed* hit rates ranging between .28 and .47 are compatible with a *true underlying probability* of .40 (because by definition, each shot had a 40% chance of success in the simulation), with some "noise" mixed in due to chance.

Notice how the conclusion I stated above included the qualifier "in the 2001 NBA postseason." If a player *really* has an inherent ability to lift his (or her) game in the postseason compared to the regular season, he/she should be able to do this in more than one season. It turns out, however, that Fisher's three-point shooting percentage in the 2000 playoffs was .41 (12 for 29), virtually identical to the roughly .40 regular-season percentage he exhibited in several seasons. And in the 2002 NBA playoffs, Fisher's percentage from behind the arc was .358 (29 of 81). In the 2002 final series against New Jersey, Fisher did shoot .667 (8-of-12) from three-point land, but as I stated above, I think it is statistically more defensible to use entire postseason records, given the very small numbers of observations in individual rounds of the playoffs. But wait! In the 2003 playoffs, Fisher's success rate on treys was .617 (29–47), suggesting that his ability to get hot in the postseason (relative to the regular season) was not, as the British say, a "one-off" phenomenon. Beyond 2003, his playoff three-point shooting percentages have not been particularly high. I have summarized these statistics in figure 10.2. Thus, I would conclude that Fisher is a fairly streaky playoff three-point shooter, but not overwhelmingly so.

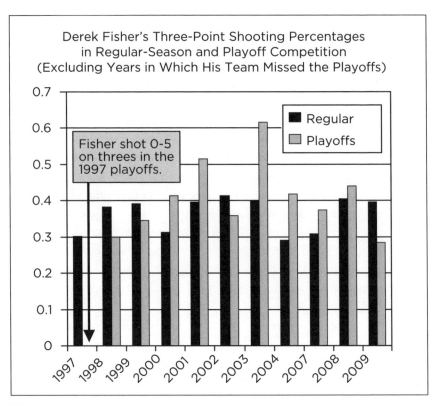

Figure 10.2

Jason McElwain was another player who probably felt like he couldn't miss. Interestingly enough, McElwain was not even a regular member of his high school team, but was thrust into the national spotlight under unusual circumstances. A local newspaper article detailed what happened to McElwain on February 15, 2006:

Jason is the trainer for the Athena varsity team. So dedicated is Jason, he has not missed a game or practice in the three years he's served the team.

Wednesday for "Senior Night," Athena coach Jim Johnson had Jason suit up for the game. He sat excitedly on the bench in his school colors. . . .

Athena moved to a comfortable 20-point lead against Spencerport. With the home crowd calling and classmates waving signs of support, Johnson called down the bench . . . Jason, headband and all, headed out onto the court. . . .

With the help of his teammates, Jason stared down a shot from the corner. The entire Athena bench, and every person in the gym rose.

Jason missed . . . by six feet.

Moments later, Jason grabbed another pass and let it rain. The shot, from beyond the three-point arc, swished straight through. In unison, those in the gym screamed.

In the game's final four minutes, Jason shot five more times from behind the three-point arc. He made them all. Each time, teammates on the bench would hold their heads and scream, fans would stomp, tears would flow.

Jason scored 20 points. He set an Athena record with a half-dozen three-pointers. His teammates and friends stormed the court. They raised him on their shoulders . . . wide-eyed and in awe of what they had seen. They asked Jason for his autograph.[19]

I would submit that, even if you assembled the nation's finest college and professional three-point shooters in a gym and had them shoot baskets with nobody defending them, it would not be easy for them to hit six straight three-pointers. Yet someone who was not even a regular member of his high school team did so! Video clips of McElwain's remarkable shooting remain widely available on the Internet.

Finally, if there were awards for Best Desperate Three-Point Barrage, they would go to Washington State in the team category for its feverish, though ultimately unsuccessful, comeback attempt against UCLA on January 12, 2008, and to Iowa's Justin Johnson in the individual category, for his single-handed (also unsuccessful) attempt to bring the Hawkeyes back against Indiana just 10 days earlier. First, here's the story of WSU's flurry. With UCLA up 68–53, the Cougars made an unbelievable *seven* three-pointers (with three different players contributing) in the final 1:37. The Bruins scored 13 points of their own in the final 1:37, including 7-of-8 free throws by Darren Collison, putting the final score at 81-74 UCLA.[20] As for Iowa's Johnson, according to an article on the game, he,

> hit six 3s in the final 1:56, each one seemingly longer than the last, to bring Iowa within two with 4.8 seconds left.
>
> "I actually thought we did a good job on him until the last two minutes. Then he went crazy," Indiana coach Kelvin Sampson said of Johnson, Iowa's top scoring threat.
>
> Johnson hit three 3s in a span of 27 seconds to bring Iowa within striking distance, and followed those up with a 40-foot bank shot with 4.8 seconds to go that sent the few remaining fans in the building into a frenzy.[21]

11

Hot Hands in Other Sports

In addition to the spectacular basketball-shooting feats discussed in the previous chapter, athletes in other sports have distinguished themselves with their streaky performances. The present chapter examines great individual performances in baseball, football, golf, and ice hockey.

BASEBALL

Next to consecutive-games hitting streaks, perhaps the most prominent type of baseball streak involves the number of straight innings a pitcher can go without allowing any runs. The major-league record, as many baseball fans will know, is held by former Los Angeles Dodger Orel Hershiser, with 59 straight scoreless innings in 1988. That year, Hershiser edged past the record set 20 years earlier by another former Dodger, Don Drysdale, at 58 2/3.[1]

Using an approach from Trent McCotter that I called the gap model (introduced in chapter 8), one could ask if there are other pitchers who would qualify for the pantheon of scoreless-streak pitching if we could (hypothetically) replace a run-scoring inning or two, here or there, with a zero. Sure enough, St. Louis Cardinal great Bob Gibson fits this category. In 1968 (starting right around the time that Drysdale's streak was ending), Gibson compiled a stretch of 47 consecutive scoreless innings. However, as baseball historians have pointed out, those 47 innings were part of a larger span of 99 innings in which Gibson allowed only two runs. On July 1, the Dodgers scored a run in the first to end Gibson's 47-inning streak. He responded by holding L.A. scoreless for the remaining eight innings, then shut out San Francisco, and followed with six scoreless innings against Houston (23 cumulative shut-out innings) before the Astros scored a run in the seventh. Undaunted, Gibson rang up another 27 innings without an opponent scoring, thus giving him 97 scoreless innings out of 99.[2] (Writer Bill Deane clarifies that the 97-of-99 scoreless-inning figure includes four shut-out innings tossed by Gibson on July 17, before the game got rained out.[3] These innings are not counted in official statistics, so some readers may prefer to credit Gibson with 93 shut-out innings out of 95.)

Skill and Luck Revisited

One of the key ideas of this book (noted in chapter 1) is that streaks often represent great skill combined with luck. An article by Jerry Crasnick in the 2007 World Series program magazine addresses in depth the sizable luck component in baseball statistics, such as batters' offensive statistics being depressed by hard-hit balls that just happen to go straight to a fielder or being enhanced by weakly hit balls that somehow sneak through to the outfield.[4] In setting his record for consecutive scoreless innings, which lasted 20 years, Drysdale benefited from one of the most controversial record-related umpiring calls in modern baseball history, which some consider a very generous piece of luck. The call occurred during an at-bat by San Francisco catcher Dick Dietz and, in fact, featured prominently in Dietz's obituary (he died in 2005 of a heart attack):

> On May 31, 1968, Dietz was batting against the Dodgers' Don Drysdale, who was working on a fifth consecutive shutout. With the bases loaded and nobody out in the ninth inning, Dietz was hit by a pitch, which would have driven in a run and ended Drysdale's streak. But umpire Harry Wendelstedt maintained that Dietz had not tried to avoid the pitch, a ruling disputed heavily by Giants manager Herman Franks, who was subsequently ejected from the game. Dietz eventually was retired, as were the next two hitters, and Drysdale's streak, which would reach a record 58 2/3 innings, continued.[5]

In addition to ability and luck (see "Skill and Luck Revisited"), another factor that may promote streakiness is the rule book. In their book *Inequality by Design*, Berkeley sociologist Claude Fischer and colleagues argued that government policies (e.g., tax rates, subsidies) play a substantial role in who "wins" and "loses" economically and materially in American society. To drive home this point, these authors use baseball rule changes as an analogy. In their historical review, "Baseball: How Rules Help Pick the Winners," Fischer and colleagues cite baseball owners' response to a "hitting drought in the mid-1960s," which included "lowering the pitching mound from fifteen to ten inches [high]."[6] Thus, in addition to their throwing ability, pitchers such as Drysdale and Gibson benefited from a *structural* feature of the game (their increased height, from getting to pitch from atop a hill, relative to batters), which baseball rule makers could shift in order to favor pitchers or hitters.

As discussed in chapter 1, streaks can be evaluated by how much room for error an athlete has in maintaining a streak. Not to take anything away from Hershiser or Drysdale, but a consecutive scoreless-innings streak allows the pitcher to give up a hit or walk here or there, without immediately ending the streak. In July of 2009, Chicago White Sox pitcher Mark Buehrle set a record for most consecutive *batters* retired, at 45.[7] For this kind of streak, any kind of result for the batter besides an out ends the stretch. Buehrle pitched a perfect game on July 23 against the Tampa Bay Rays—27 batters up and 27 down— only the 18th perfect game in major-league history (at the time). He then came back five days later and mowed down the first 17 Minnesota Twins he faced, before allowing a base-runner (Minnesota then started hitting Buehrle and won the game). Adding in an out from the last batter from the start before the perfect game, that's where you get the total of 45 straight batters retired. Before Buehrle's spurt of hotness, the record had been shared by his White Sox teammate Bobby Jenks (in 2007) and former San Francisco Giant Jim Barr (in 1972) at 41. It strikes me (no pun intended) as an interesting question whether a long streak of consecutive batters retired would be easier to accomplish as a starter (such as Buehrle) or as a reliever (such as Jenks). A starter can, of course, build up the streak in fewer games, but must have the stamina to keep pitching at a high level throughout the game. A reliever, on the other hand, may know that he is only going to pitch an inning or two on a given night, which would allow him to concentrate on retiring just a few opposing batters (going "all guns a'blazing" with each one). A reliever, though, would have to keep this up for perhaps 20, 30, or more appearances to contend for this record. I say it's harder for the reliever!

As discussed in some of the earlier chapters, a key issue in the debate over streakiness and momentum concerns how to interpret a player's (or team's) stretch of performance that exceeds (or falls below) the player's (or team's) prior record. If, for example, a pitcher with a prior long-term earned run average

(ERA) of 4.25 goes his next few starts limiting the opponents to 3.10 earned runs per nine innings, does the change represent chance variation (like a long streak of heads in coin-flipping) or a real, substantive improvement in the pitcher's proficiency? Statistical research has found rises and falls in athletes' performances to be consistent with chance (i.e., coin-flipping) fluctuations, for the most part. Having said this, one does encounter from time to time situations in which it appears a player or team *really* has shown an elevation in performance.

In May 2008, the Houston Astros' Lance Berkman went on an offensive *tear*. More impressive than the length of his hot streak (which wasn't bad) was the magnitude of it. According to a May 18, 2008, article on the Astros' game against the Texas Rangers, "Lance Berkman was 2-of-5 to keep his [seasonal] average at .399. Berkman is on a 17-game hitting streak in which he is 36-of-66 [an average of .545] with eight home runs and 21 RBIs." Further, with 36 hits in the 17 games, he was averaging more than two hits per game (2.12). Finally, Berkman's slugging percentage in his most recent seven games going back from May 18 (.962) exceeded his career figure (.568) by nearly .400 points.[8]

An arguably more impressive instance of performance-lifting was Fresno State's rise in 2008 from being the number 89–ranked college baseball team entering the postseason (per a statistic known as the RPI) to winning the NCAA national championship. This one just *seems* too momentous to attribute to random variation. According to a *Baseball America* column, "Statistically, Fresno's the biggest upset winner in [College World Series] history, perhaps all of college sports history."[9] To dramatize the point, ESPN television announcers noted that another underdog that had captured U.S. sports fans' imagination—George Mason University's 2006 men's final four basketball team—had an RPI ranking much better than that of the Fresno State baseballers, namely number 26.

After finishing the regular season with a 33–27 record (21–11 in the Western Athletic Conference), Fresno State proceeded to go 4–0 in the WAC tournament, 3–1 in an NCAA regional hosted by highly regarded Long Beach State, 2–1 at highly ranked Arizona State in the super-regionals, and 5–2 in the College World Series; one CWS loss occurred in pool play, and the other in the two-out-of-three title round. All told, playing against many of the nation's top teams, Fresno State went 14–4 in the postseason. In addition to some top-shelf pitching, Fresno State showed robust offensive production, scoring a CWS record-tying 62 runs.

Back-to-Back-to-Back-to-Back . . .

A dramatic but rare type of baseball streak is when consecutive batters hit home runs. If two straight hitters send balls over the fence, that will capture people's attention. But when the number of consecutive homers exceeds two, fans surely will realize they're witnessing something pretty amazing. The feat of four straight homers by a team has been accomplished seven times in MLB history, four times between 2006 and 2010 and three times from 1961 to 1964.[10] In college baseball, South Carolina hit five in a row on June 10, 2006, which tied the record for that level of play.[11] The Los Angeles Dodgers' 2006 outburst, presumably because it was MLB's first in 42 years, garnered extensive media coverage. The *Wall Street Journal*'s "Numbers Guy," Carl Bialik, asked some prominent statisticians to look into the probability of the Dodgers' accomplishment and I offered my two cents' worth on my Hot Hand website. Essentially, one would take the home-run probability of each player involved in the streak, and then multiply these figures all together. Depending on factors such as whether one uses plate appearances or official at-bats as the denominator to determine players' home-run percentages, one comes up with estimates ranging from roughly 1-in-500,000 to 1-in-3 million for the Dodgers' four straight shots. (Plate appearances might be preferable, but players who frequently get walked intentionally or "pitched around" might have their home-run prowess underestimated, relative to official at-bats.) Further, taking into account the multiple opportunities in a season a team has to put together a stretch of four home runs, the likelihood might be as low as 1-in-100. Another factor to consider, mentioned earlier in the book, is "streak pitching." In this case, a given pitcher might not have his best "stuff" going and might also be unable to vary the location of his pitches. In some of the above streaks, however, the opposing teams changed pitchers midway through the barrages.

FOOTBALL

Many of the most noteworthy football streaks put a premium on staying healthy enough to play in a long stretch of games, given the brutality out on the field. As shown in the table at the end of this chapter, two leading records are quarterback Brett Favre's consecutive starts and receiver Jerry Rice's streak for consecutive games with at least one catch; while skill is certainly not absent (or else Favre and Rice would have been benched at some time), these records seem heavily based on longevity in the game. Two other records add more of a skill component to longevity: Johnny Unitas's streak of consecutive games with at least one touchdown pass, and running-back Barry Sanders's streak of rushing for 100-or-more yards in 14 straight games.

One of the few positions in football that doesn't have much of a physical longevity component is place-kicker. In 2003, the Indianapolis Colts' Mike Vanderjagt made *all* 37 of his regular-season field-goal attempts.[12] This is one of those cases where you can only assume a prior probability to conduct analyses (otherwise you would have to use his seasonal hit rate of 1.00). I found that even assuming a 90 percent chance of success on each kick, the likelihood of Vanderjagt's making them all was only 2-in-100, based on $(.9)^{37}$. This calculation does not take into account the distance of each attempt. Obviously, the more distant the attempts, the more impressive the streak would be. It took another streak, of sorts, to get me to conduct a more distance-sensitive analysis. . . .

On the afternoon of October 21, 2007, the Tennessee Titans at Houston Texans game had two major streakiness story lines. Houston, trailing 32–7 entering the fourth quarter, went on a 29–3 burst in the final period to take a 36–35 lead with 57 seconds remaining. Tennessee moved the ball down the field in the closing moments, however, to set up kicker Rob Bironas (the other streaky story of the day) for a game-winning 29-yard field goal as time ran out. The "hot-footed" Bironas's winning kick was his eighth successful field goal of the game, setting a new NFL record (he had no misses).[13] The yardage distances of the field goals in the order in which they occurred are as follows:

52, 25, 21, 30, 28, 43, 29, 29

Looking at Bironas's career field-goal accuracy statistics, broken down by distance of the attempt, they were as follows, at the time (I chose to use career statistics rather than just those from 2007 in order to achieve a larger sample size):

20–29 yards 21/23 (.91)
30–39 yards 18/19 (.95)
40–49 yards 11/18 (.61)
50+ yards 3/7 (.43)

To estimate the probability of Bironas's making all eight field-goal attempts he took, given that he would be receiving these opportunities, we multiply the component probabilities together:

(.43) (.91) (.91) (.95) (.91) (.61) (.91) (.91)

This yields .155. If we also factored in the likelihood of an NFL team having so many drives stall in fairly close proximity to the goal line, the probability of Bironas's accomplishment would probably get even smaller.

A couple of cautions are in order about this analysis. First, it is the unusual nature of the feat (or in this case, foot) that drew me to conduct the analysis; I did not seek a random cross-section of games. Second, as is the case for many of the analyses displayed throughout this book, my calculation assumed independence of observations, that the outcome of any one kick had no impact on the next. As I like to remind readers periodically, the independence assumption is typically associated with sequences of coin flips and dice rolling, which unlike humans, cannot experience momentum and other associated psychological states. However, having conducted numerous analyses over the years for my website and read ones conducted by others, I consider the independence assumption to hold pretty well for athletic performances, too.

GOLF

Among golf's illustrious figures, the two names that dominate discussions of streakiness are Tiger Woods and Byron Nelson. For consecutive PGA tournament wins, Nelson holds the record (achieved in 1945) with 11, whereas Woods is in second place with 7 (accomplished from 2006 to 2007).[14] When it comes to consecutive times making the cut (playing well enough in a tournament's first two rounds to qualify for the third and fourth rounds and, ultimately, a paycheck), Woods holds the record at 142, with Nelson second at 113.[15] Of all these marks, it is Nelson's record of 11 straight tournament wins that, in my view, warrants the most attention. That year (1945), Nelson won 18 tournaments in all and came in second seven times.[16] Not bad for someone who played in 30 tournaments for the year!

My first thought about Nelson was that his primary feat was winning 18 tournaments in a single year (that's undeniable), from which the streak of 11 straight would more-or-less automatically follow. When someone wins such a high percentage of the time, long streaks are virtually inevitable, as there are relatively few non-win events to break up the streaks. Imagine 30 small boxes laid out in a row, representing the 30 tournaments Nelson entered in 1945. Further, imagine 18 little W-shaped objects, each representing one of Nelson's tournament wins that year:

W W W W W W W W W W W W W W W W W W

□□□□□ □□□□□ □□□□□ □□□□□ □□□□□ □□□□□

How many ways are there to deposit 18 W's in 30 receptacles? A lot. For example, the W's could go in the first 18 boxes, or they could go in boxes 1 and 2 then 4 through 19. Or in boxes 13 through 30, or in boxes 1, 2, 5, 7, 8, 11, 12, 13, 19, 20, 21, 22, 23, 24, 26, 27, 28, and 30. And so forth. I thought it would be interesting to document all the possible ways 18 wins could be distributed sequentially into 30 boxes (tournaments) and then see what percent of the time a winning streak of 11 or greater occurred. The first part—figuring out how many possible ways 18 objects can be distributed into 30 slots—involves a well-known mathematical principle called "n choose k," or in this case, "30 choose 18." Interested readers can consult an introductory statistics or probability book, or check online, to learn more about the "n choose k" principle (also known as the binomial coefficient).

I obtained the solution to "30 choose 18" and it informs us that there are 86,493,225 ways to arrange 18 objects in 30 boxes. Rather than list them all, therefore, I decided it would be easier to do simulations. Borrowing a page from Trent McCotter (see chapter 3), I started out with a listing of all numbers from 1 to 30. Any number from 1 to 18 would symbolize a "win," whereas any number from 19 to 30 would represent a non-win. I then used a website (http://www.random.org/sequences) to take the numbers 1–30 and sort them randomly, 100 different times (also known as taking *permutations*). One example of these random sequences is as follows:

30, 25, 24, **13, 16, 12, 2, 14,** 29, 7, 5, 11, 8, 26, 1, 21, 15, 3, 20, 19, 27, 23, 9, 10, 22, 18, 28, 6, 17, 4

All winning streaks (i.e., streaks of numbers 18 and lower) are underlined. The longest streak observed in this sequence (5 straight wins) is bolded as well. My initial thinking, again, is that winning streaks of 11 straight tournaments would flow readily, *given that Nelson had won 18 out of 30 tournaments.* As it turned out, there was only one streak of 11 straight wins in my 100 random simulations, along with one of 10 straight wins, and 4 of 9 straight wins. So, yes, a streak of 11 straight wins (or thereabouts) can occur by random in the midst of winning 18 tournaments total out of 30 for the year, but not as frequently as I would have guessed.

An Unusual Golf Streak

Right here in Lubbock, at Texas Tech University's Rawls golf course (located about a mile and a half from my office), a 53-year-old gentleman named Danny Leake shot a hole-in-one at the same hole (the sixth) two days in a row the weekend of July 29 and 30, 2006. According to an article in the local newspaper, the hole had distances of 174 and 178 yards the two days, differing as a result of pin placement on the green.[17] Naturally, I felt compelled to estimate the probability of what Leake had done, and I was aided in my calculations by previous hole-in-one probability estimates (taking into account distance to the hole and player ability level) published by *Golf Digest*. The steps in my calculation were pretty elaborate and the final estimate I came up with was 1 in 1.75 billion! The full details of what I did are available online in the July 31, 2006, entry of my Hot Hand blog.

ICE HOCKEY

The night was October 31, 2008. Fittingly for Halloween, the goaltenders for the Vancouver Canucks and Anaheim (Mighty) Ducks had to keep their masks on longer than usual. Tied 6–6 after regulation, the teams played a five-minute overtime period, but there was no scoring. The game then went to a shootout, a sequence of one-on-one shooter-goalie encounters with the teams alternating roles. Vancouver won the shootout, two goals to one, resulting in an official 7–6 final score.[18] This was far from a normal shootout, however!

According to protocol, each team fielded three shooters to go up against the other team's goalie, analogous to a three-inning baseball game. If two teams are tied after the initial three rounds—which was the case between Vancouver and Anaheim—then an "extra-innings" system is used. As soon as one team scores in a round and the other team doesn't, the game is over. After the Canucks and Ducks completed the main three-round shootout tied at a goal apiece, one extra round after another kept passing by with neither team able to score. Here is a line score of the shootout I created (Table 11.1) from a narrative summary[19] I found online:

	1	2	3	4	5	6	7	8	9	10	11	12	13	T
Ducks	0	1	0	0	0	0	0	0	0	0	0	0	0	1
Canucks	1	0	0	0	0	0	0	0	0	0	0	0	1	2

That's right, the shootout lasted for 13 rounds! Both goalies—Vancouver's Roberto Luongo and Anaheim's Jonas Hiller—sparkled in the shootout. Luongo was beaten only once by the Ducks in the shootout, whereas Hiller stopped 11 straight Canuck shots before giving up the game-winner. (Unsuccessful attempts can be divided into saves, shots that would have gone in but for the presence of the goalie, and misses, shots that were off-target wide or high. I would argue that goalies still deserve some credit for misses, as good goaltending likely induces shooters to take risky shots, such as aiming for corners of the net.)

The question I decided to pursue was as follows: given these goalies' prior success rates, what was the probability of each netminder doing as well as he did in the Halloween Night shootout? In conducting this analysis, I was aided greatly by the amazing website NHLShootouts.com, which provides extensive, up-to-date data on shootouts. Hiller did not have a lot of experience in shootouts; other than Halloween 2008, he participated only in three shootouts the previous season, giving up 5 goals in 12 shots overall. The NHL Shootouts website gives Hiller a save percentage of .583 (evidently not distinguishing saves from misses). I then asked how likely it was that a goalie with a prior .583 success rate could stop 11 (or more) shots out of 13, using the online calculator discussed in chapter 2. The answer came to a probability of approximately .05, a level social scientists would traditionally consider "statistically significant" (i.e., highly unlikely to have occurred simply by chance). Over the three preceding seasons, Luongo had participated in 30 shootouts, compiling a cumulative success rate of .714. For a goalie with such a percentage to rebuff 12 (or more) shots out of 13 yields a probability of .08. Another way to look at this finding is that Luongo is a better shootout (if not overall) goalie than Hiller (albeit based on small sample sizes), so Luongo's stellar shootout performance would be less surprising. For the record, the Halloween 2008 Canuck-Duck marathon was not the longest shootout since the NHL started using it as an ultimate tie-breaker in the 2005–2006 season. The record is at least 15 rounds, from a November 2005 contest (the score was 4–3 within the shootout).

Consistent with the preceding example, talk of streakiness in hockey usually centers on the notion of the "hot goalie." Perhaps because goals are so rare, it's hard to envision a streak *shooter* in hockey. Goalies, on the other hand, face large numbers of shots, cumulatively, over long stretches of games, so hot performances can be detected readily. Not too many years ago, a major goaltending record was broken as Brian Boucher, playing for the Phoenix Coyotes, set an NHL record with 332 consecutive scoreless minutes (the equivalent of over five complete regulation games, where he made 146 consecutive saves). Quoting from an online biography:

> On January 11, 2004, the streak finally ended for Boucher. At 6:16 of the first period, in Phoenix's home game against the Atlanta Thrashers, Randy Robitaille fired a slap shot from the blue line which glanced off the chest of Phoenix defenseman David Tanabe and into the net. "I don't think it would have hit the net if it didn't hit me," Tanabe said. "It if wasn't for that bounce, he could have had another shutout." With the deflection, Boucher had no time to react and block the shot. "A fluky goal," he said. "That's how easily a goal can go in. The fact that it didn't happen for five-plus games is pretty amazing."[20]

That last quote captures it all, as far as I'm concerned. Boucher was obviously playing at a high level during the streak (along, presumably, with his team's defensemen, whose job it was to hinder opponents' scoring chances). However, a sizable amount of luck had to be thrown into the mix to make a streak like Boucher's possible. I follow hockey moderately closely, I would say, and I hadn't heard much about Boucher in the years following his streak. I did a little research and found that, after the 2004–2005 NHL season was lost due to the owners' lockout, Boucher's career went into an apparent decline. He played in only 59 total NHL games in the four seasons from 2005–2006 to 2008–2009, moving around between several different teams (although he made a comeback of sorts with the 2009–2010 Stanley Cup runner-up Philadelphia Flyers). Boucher would thus appear to be a counterexample to the pattern of many record streaks belonging to all-time great athletes in a sport (e.g., Joe DiMaggio, Tiger Woods).

One final perspective on the issue of "hot goalies" is whether there are some netminders who appear to raise their level of stinginess in the Stanley Cup playoffs, relative to the regular season. The 2003 NHL Stanley Cup playoffs featured some of the best goaltending in recent history, in the name of Anaheim's Jean-Sebastien Giguere and New Jersey's Martin Brodeur, each of whom led his team to the Stanley Cup finals. Though Brodeur's Devils ended up besting Giguere's Mighty Ducks in a seven-game final, it was Giguere (or as he came to be known, "Jiggy") who received greater attention during the playoffs; Giguere also won the Conn Smythe Trophy, signifying the most valuable player in the playoffs.

Giguere came to notice early in the playoffs, as Anaheim stunned the defending champion Detroit Red Wings in a first-round sweep (four games to none). Then, after a 4–2 Anaheim series win over the highly regarded Dallas Stars, the Mighty Ducks found themselves up in the Western Conference finals against another "Cinderella," the Minnesota Wild (a recent expansion team). It was against Minnesota that Giguere *really* got hot. He became the first goalie since 1945 to shut out the opposing team in the first three games of a playoff series. Minnesota finally did score in game 4, however, ending Giguere's scoreless streak at 217 minutes, 54 seconds![21] (For those of you who are not big ice hockey fans, a regulation game is 60 minutes, with sudden-death overtime lasting as long as necessary in the playoffs.) Once the finals started, it was Brodeur who was the hot goalie, however, as the Devils shut out the Ducks by identical 3–0 scores in games 1 and 2. Jiggy suddenly looked human, but he recovered. Anaheim evened the series, with Giguere besting Brodeur in a 1–0 overtime thriller in game 4. The two teams split the next two games, which were high-scoring, but in the decisive game 7, it was Brodeur getting the better of things with yet another 3–0 shut-out.

Once all the games were over and the champion Devils skated the Stanley Cup around the rink in celebration, I tried to document in some statistical sense the hot-goalie phenomenon, where a netminder substantially elevates his performance in the playoffs and leads his team into championship contention. Specifically, I looked for instances of goalies' lowering their goals-against-averages (GAA; defined by ESPN.com's NHL Statistics Glossary as "the number of non-empty net goals allowed by a goalie per 60 minutes") substantially in the playoffs, compared to the regular season. For context, any time a goalie keeps his GAA below 2.00, it is considered very good. To try to distinguish transient vs. true "hotness," statisticians have suggested checking whether athletes who exhibited streakiness one year are able to do it again in later years. At the time, I conducted some fairly elaborate statistical analyses comparing the 2003 playoffs with those of 2002 and 2001, but they didn't appear to yield a clear message. Thus, I'll just present a very basic summary.

During the three years studied, a couple of goalies demonstrated what might be called "isolated hotness." In 2002, Arturs Irbe lowered his GAA by .87 from the regular season (2.54) to the playoffs (1.67), in leading the Carolina Hurricanes to the Stanley Cup finals; in 2001, however, he actually did worse in the playoffs than in the regular season (he was not in the playoffs in 2003). Longtime Montreal Canadiens and Colorado Avalanche goalie Patrick Roy, considered by many the finest NHL goaltender of all time, lowered his GAA by .51 (2.21 regular-season; 1.70 playoffs) in leading the 2001 Avalanche to the Stanley Cup. In 2002 and 2003, Roy's playoff GAA values were slightly higher than his respective regular-season marks, but the latter were already at very low levels (1.94 in 2002, and 2.18 in 2003).

Within the same years, two goalies displayed "repeated hotness." The aforementioned Brodeur, who also draws a lot of votes for greatest NHL goaltender, lowered his GAA from the regular season to the playoffs in all three of the years studied. Most notably, Brodeur recorded playoff GAA's of 1.42 in 2002 (compared to 2.15 in the regular season) and 1.65 in 2003 (compared to 2.02 in the regular season). The other goalie to demonstrate sustained playoff hotness is Patrick Lalime, then playing for Ottawa. In 2002, his playoff GAA (1.39) was *more than a full goal* better than his regular-season mark of 2.48, whereas in 2003, his playoff GAA of 1.82 was modestly better than his regular-season mark of 2.16. Like the aforementioned Brian Boucher, Lalime has had his ups and downs since his years of peak brilliance, but he remains in the NHL. Finally, we have Giguere, who shined in the 2003 postseason (1.62 GAA, compared to 2.30 in the regular season). He did not participate in the 2001 or 2002 playoffs, so I couldn't analyze his year-to-year hotness in my original study. Giguere has remained with the Ducks and in 2007, had a nice playoff run (1.97 GAA compared to 2.26 in the regular season) as Anaheim won the Stanley Cup.

Streakiness in Chess?

Interest in streakiness is not limited to major sports, the kind that frequently appear on television such as basketball, baseball, football, tennis, and golf. Streak-related themes have even permeated the game of chess. While attending the biennial U.S. Conference on Teaching Statistics, at the Ohio State University, I noticed an interesting headline in the local newspaper, the *Columbus Dispatch*. It read: "Slumps Uncommon in Royal Game." Spurred by discussion of baseball slumps, chess writer Shelby Lyman drew the following comparison: "The complex body mechanics required for [pitching or hitting a baseball] are easily thrown off for weeks or months. In contrast, top chess players rarely have prolonged down periods in performance. One likely reason is the negligible physical component in chess. Motor responses gone awry seem intrinsically more difficult to correct than poorly tuned decision making."[22]

As I did in chapter 9 with team streaks, I will conclude this chapter with a table to acknowledge a number of outstanding individual-sport streaks that I did not discuss in the main text.

Ratings of Top Individual Streaks

	Fox Sports TV "The Sports List" (August 31, 2004)	ESPN.com Jeff Merron (May 2005)	Allen St. John* Made to Be Broken (2006)
Joe DiMaggio: 56-game hitting streak (1941)	1	1	4
Cal Ripken Jr.: 2,632 consecutive baseball games played (1982–1998)	2	5	50
Brett Favre: 297 consecutive NFL starts (1992–2010)	3	10	—
Orel Hershiser: 59 straight scoreless innings (1988)	4	4	—
Pitcher Greg Maddux: consecutive years recorded 15 or more wins (17 straight seasons by end of 2004)	5	—	—
Reliever Eric Gagne succeeds in 84 straight save chances (2002–2004)	6	—	—
NHL goalie Brian Boucher: five consecutive shutouts, 332 scoreless minutes (2003–2004)	7	—	47
Edwin Moses, 400-meter hurdler: wins 107 straight final races (1977–1987)	8	2	—
Barry Sanders: running for 100+ yards in 14 straight NFL games (1997)	9	—	—
NFL receiver Jerry Rice: straight games with at least one catch (ended at 274 on September 19, 2004)	10	—	—
Pitcher Anthony Young: 27 straight losses (1992–1993)	HM	—	—
Lance Armstrong: 7 straight Tour de France bicycling wins (1999–2005)	—	3	41
Johnny Unitas: 47 games with at least one touchdown pass (1956–1960)	—	6	16

	Fox Sports TV "The Sports List" (August 31, 2004)	ESPN.com Jeff Merron (May 2005)	Allen St. John* *Made to Be Broken* (2006)
Rocky Marciano: 49-0 heavyweight boxing record (1947-1956)	—	7	—
Cael Sanderson: 159-0 college wrestling record (1999-2002)	—	8	—
NHL great Wayne Gretzky: getting a goal or assist in 51 straight games (1983-1984)	—	9	—
Johnny Vander Meer: two consecutive no-hitters pitched (1938)	—	—	11
Tiger Woods: making the cut in 142 straight golf tourneys (1998-2005)	—	—	24
Martina Navratilova: winning 74 straight singles tennis matches (1984)	—	—	27
Byron Nelson: winning 11 straight golf tourneys (1945)	—	—	38

*St. John's book lists sports accomplishments, including streaks and other records (e.g., career number of home runs). HM = Honorable Mention

III
Cold Streaks and Oddities

12

Cold Streaks

In addition to the long streaks of brilliant performance just discussed, teams and individuals can also experience disastrous streaks, where they fail again and again and again. There is an important structural difference in the opportunities for individual athletes to produce long streaks of positive (e.g., made baskets, hits in baseball) and negative (missed shots, hitless at-bats) performance, however. Winning streaks theoretically have no limit. With losing streaks, on the other hand, there's a real chance a team will bench (or release) a player who is not doing well, thus cutting off opportunities for streaks of poor performance to get too long. Still, some athletes manage to put together long stretches of futility anyway. In team sports, there is no structural impediment to long losing streaks in the United States. Other countries, though, use a system known as *demotion* or *relegation*, where teams finishing at the bottom of the standings of a higher-ability league are sent down to a lower-ability league for the next season (and top teams from lower-level leagues get promoted to a more competitive league). Soccer's English Premier League is one place such a promotion/relegation system is used.[1]

I noted earlier (chapter 1) that records for successful sports performances tended to be held by athletes who, independent of their streaks, would be considered among the greatest all-time players in their respective sports (e.g., Joe DiMaggio, Tiger Woods). Conversely, long streaks of failure occur most readily to teams and individuals who are poorly positioned to compete with better-established opponents. For example, when the NFL's Tampa Bay Buccaneers lost 26 straight games spanning 1976 and 1977, it was when they were a new expansion team. In the case of the Prairie View A&M college football team, which lost 80 straight games over the course of a decade (1989–1998), the team's lack of resources, as described in Rosabeth Moss Kanter's book *Confidence*, seemed to make winning a near-impossibility:

Football practices were held in a lopsided intramural field because the athletic department couldn't afford to get the fields mowed. Wearing Houston Oilers' hand-me-down practice pants, players walked from a dingy basement locker room to practice. . . . There were no goalposts on that field, and no coaching towers. The kickers practiced extra points against a softball backstop. The water fountain was a garden hose.[2]

Losing under such dire circumstances is not surprising. To me, therefore, the most interesting losing/failure streaks are those that occur to athletes and teams that have shown some ability to do well (not that I take pleasure in these athletes' distress). This chapter examines a number of losing (and other poor-performance) streaks, some more famous than others.

If you were a baseball fan in the early 1990s, you almost certainly would have heard of New York Mets' pitcher Anthony Young. The right-hander compiled a major-league record 27-straight losses spanning the 1992 and 1993 seasons (the previous record dated back to 1910–1911).[3] Why would a team retain a pitcher like that and continue to send him to the mound (in Young's case, about equally often as a starter and a reliever)? One thing is that whether a pitcher officially gets a Win or a Loss (or a No Decision) for a game depends only partly on how well he pitched. A pitcher can throw very effectively, limiting the opposition to, say, one run, but if the pitcher's team doesn't score at all, that pitcher will receive an "L" (see the official rules in "Determining a Baseball Game's Official Winning and Losing Pitchers"). Related to the previous point, Young indeed pitched well in some of his appearances, but either lost or failed to win via circumstances outside of his control.

A June 2, 1993, *New York Times* article carried the headline: "Don't Pin This Loss on Young."[4] The article described how, "Young, an emergency starter, had shut out the Cubs for six innings. He had allowed three hits and struck out four, and departed [for a pinch-hitter] with a 1–0 lead and the admiration of the manager." Ultimately, the Met pitchers who relieved Young were feckless, resulting in an 8–3 Cub win. Young didn't get the loss —that went to one of the Met pitchers who came in after him —but neither did he get the win that would have halted his losing streak. The *Times* article characterized thusly what Young had to show for the game: "His chance at his first victory in more than a year squashed, his six innings of virtual perfection wasted and worthless. His streak of consecutive defeats remained at 19."

About a month later (July 8, 1993), a *New York Times* story about Young's appearance vs. San Diego opened this way: "It was the best stuff that Anthony

Young has, the best he has thrown during this whole miserable 14-month losing streak. He threw strikes. He retired batter after batter. There was one simple single, from San Diego's leadoff hitter, and then Young set down 23 straight Padres yesterday."[5] Young ultimately gave up a two-run homer, however, and with the Mets getting shut out, Young absorbed his 26th straight loss, by a 2–0 score.

Determining a Baseball Game's Official Winning and Losing Pitchers

The official Major League Baseball rules (available at mlb.com) state: "The official scorer shall credit as the winning pitcher that pitcher whose team assumes a lead while such pitcher is in the game, or during the inning on offense in which such pitcher is removed from the game, and does not relinquish such lead, unless . . . a starting pitcher . . . has not completed . . . five innings of a game that lasts six or more innings." The rules state further that "a losing pitcher is a pitcher who is responsible for the run that gives the winning team a lead that the winning team does not relinquish."

On the evening of November 28, 2008, the University of Dayton men's basketball team—though ultimately winning its game against Auburn, 60–59— went 0-for-24 on three-pointers.[6] As a result, the following entry from the NCAA basketball record book had to be erased:

THREE-POINT FIELD-GOAL ATTEMPTS WITHOUT
MAKING ONE
22—Canisius vs. St. Bonaventure, Jan. 21, 1995[7]

Dayton entered the Auburn game hitting from behind the arc at a .395 clip (for purposes of the calculations to come, the same figure can be expressed as a .605 failure rate, i.e., one minus the success rate).

To estimate the probability of a team with the Flyers' previous success rate going 0-for-24 on three-point attempts, we simply raise .605 to the 24th power, yielding .000006 or 6-in-1 million. Again, this analysis assumes *independence of observations*, that the outcome of one Dayton shot has no bearing on the next, like coin flips. Though reasons can be generated for why basketball shots should not be independent—such as confidence, momentum, or fatigue—sports performances have tended to be consistent with an independence model.

One reason a team might have such a disastrous night is that it fell way behind and jacked up a lot of desperation three-point attempts. This does not
appear to be true of the Dayton situation, however, as the Auburn game appears to have been close throughout; the Flyers led 26–21 at the half and won
in overtime. Another line of inquiry is whether the lion's share of Dayton's
trey attempts somehow were taken disproportionately by the team's weakest
shooters from long distance, thus rendering the aforementioned .395 baseline
inappropriate. Looking once again at the Flyers' pre-Auburn stats, Dayton's
top three-point shooters coming in were Marcus Johnson, .500 (7–14);
Mickey Perry, .455 (5–11); Chris Johnson, .417 (5–12); and Luke Fabrizius,
.412 (7–17). According to the box score of the Dayton-Auburn contest, this
quartet took 13 of the team's 24 shots, so the Flyers' best long-distance shooters
appear to have been reasonably well represented.

As astronomical as these odds appear to be, huge streaks of missed three-
pointers haven't been all that uncommon in recent years. On February 21,
2009, the Oklahoma State women went 0–18 from behind the arc against
Texas Tech,[8] whereas on December 10, 2005, the Kentucky men missed their
first 20 three-point attempts vs. Indiana (going 2-of-27 in all).[9] Talking about
Kentucky, that's a good lead-in to the next section . . . .

With the completion of the 2010 horse racing season, it has been 32 years
since a horse has won the Triple Crown (i.e., winning the Kentucky Derby,
Preakness Stakes, and Belmont Stakes in the same year).[10] These races are only
for three-year-olds, so a given horse can only make one attempt at the Triple
Crown. In my earliest years as a sports fan, approaching the age of 10 in the
early 1970s, perhaps the most salient fact about horse racing was that no horse
since Citation in 1948 had won the Triple Crown. Then, in a dramatic turnaround, we had three Triple Crown winners in short succession: Secretariat
(1973), Seattle Slew (1977), and Affirmed (1978). I wondered, what's so difficult about winning the Triple Crown? The pendulum then swung back the
other way, where Triple Crowns again became extremely elusive.

I started writing about the Triple Crown drought after the 2004 Belmont.
Heading into that race, it looked like the dry spell would end. Smarty Jones,
a horse who captured the nation's imagination like no other in recent years,
had not only won the Kentucky Derby and Preakness; he had never lost in
any race, and had won the first two legs of the Triple Crown rather decisively
(especially the Preakness, by 11½ lengths). But it was not to be, as Smarty
Jones was edged out in the Belmont by longshot Birdstone. Once more since

then, in 2008, there was the possibility of a Triple Crown after the first two races, as Big Brown had won the Kentucky Derby and Preakness, but he faltered badly in the Belmont.

From the perspective of statistical analysis and streakiness, the question that most prominently surfaced in my mind was this: given the frequency of horses' winning the Triple Crown prior to 1979, what was the probability of having no Triple Crown winners from 1979 onward? There have been 11 Triple Crown winners in history (again, the latest in 1978). The year 1875 was the first in which all three races were held, giving us a rate of 11/104 or .106 between 1875 and 1978. A .106 rate of winning the Triple Crown prior to 1979 translates into a .894 rate of *not winning* the Triple Crown. As a simple estimate of the probability of going 32 straight years (1979–2010) without a Triple Crown, we can take $(.894)^{32} = .03$. Thus, at the beginning of the 32-year interval from 1979 to 2010, there would have been only a 3 percent chance of having no Triple Crown winners during this time, but yet that's what's happened. In other words, there would have been a very high likelihood of at least one Triple Crown winner in the last 32 years. This calculation, of course, assumes *independence* of outcomes from year to year, which fits well with attempts to win the Triple Crown, as the horses are different each year (although the jockeys and trainers may be the same).

My 2004 Hot Hand blog posting on the Triple Crown drought (which does not appear on the current blog because I switched hosting sites in 2006) attracted an unusual amount of commentary. The comments varied from being statistically focused to addressing horses' breeding and physical properties. Regarding the latter line of inquiry, it helps to know that the Belmont Stakes is 1½ miles long, a good deal longer than the Kentucky Derby and Preakness (1¼ miles and 1 3/16 miles, respectively).

University of Alberta professor Ric Johnson wondered, "What is the chance we would not have a Triple Crown in ten occasions where a horse wins the first two legs?" (which is how many such failures have occurred from 1979 to 2004). Noted Johnson, "I count 11 Triple Crown winners of 21 opportunities (winners of the first two legs) up to 1978, for a probability of .52381." Given that .52381 is the Triple Crown success rate given wins by the same horse in the first two races, up to 1978, we take 1 – .52381 = .47619 to get the failure rate. "Taking this [latter] number to the tenth power, you get a likelihood of .0006 for getting no Triple Crowns in ten opportunities since 1978."

Noting that, "One of my highest grades at UCLA was in statistics and I have probably cleaned more stalls than most of your correspondents," my uncle Irving Reifman from Los Angeles contended that, "horses are bred and raced much differently in the last 20 years, with more emphasis on speed at shorter distances. Lasix, a diuretic, is commonly used to inhibit bleeding from the lungs, but has probably weakened the current breed. In fact, thoroughbred racing has seen almost no new speed records in 20 years, while harness times dropped dramatically. Finally, there are 3 or 4 times as many big purses for 2-year-olds and pre-Derby 3-year-olds as before. All this early racing weakens, not strengthens, the breed. After all, you can't compare pole-vault records to those prior to the flexible pole."

Gambling researcher Nigel Turner from the Centre for Addiction and Mental Health in Toronto also focused on biological factors in horse breeding. He suggested that, "the quality of race horse is creeping upwards as a result of selective breeding and the genetics of the horses is becoming more and more homogenous. . . . Today, the horses are genetically very homogeneous and thus large differences in ability are less likely to occur. Racing today may be more random (less influenced by differential ability) than it was in the past."

13

Unusual Streaks (Neither Hot nor Cold)

The 2005–2006 St. Louis University (SLU) men's basketball team opened up its season on November 22, 2005, with a win over Eastern Illinois. The Billikens then lost at Hawaii on November 27 to even out their record at 1–1. SLU won its next game, then lost the game after that. Then it won its next game, but lost its game after that. You've probably detected a pattern: win, lose, win, lose, win, lose, and so forth. St. Louis did exactly that, alternating wins and losses for its first 19 games of the season! After a victory over Fordham on January 28, 2006, SLU's record stood at 10–9. The Billikens then won at Rhode Island on February 1, marking the first time St. Louis had won (or lost) two games in a row.[1] Just like that, the streak of alternating one win and one loss was over.

To estimate the probability of an alternation streak like St. Louis's, we need to revisit the "*n* choose *k*" concept, introduced in chapter 11 in connection with golfing great Byron Nelson. We can say that we have 19 boxes, corresponding to the 19 games for which SLU maintained the alternation of wins and losses. We know further that the Billikens won exactly 10 of those games. The way St. Louis distributed its 10 wins—putting them in every odd-numbered game—is but one way to distribute 10 objects in 19 boxes. SLU could have won games 1–10, or games 1–5 and 15–19, or games 2, 3, 5, 6, 9, 11, 14, 16, 18, and 19. Using the expression "19 choose 10," we find that there were 92,378 ways the 10 wins could have occurred in 19 games, thus making the way St. Louis did it seem pretty rare indeed!

One might argue that, for whatever reason, maybe St. Louis's schedule was arranged so that games against "easy" opponents alternated with ones against "hard" opponents. That may account for part of what happened as, for example, SLU's sixth game (where the team exhibited a pattern of losing even-numbered games) was at perennial powerhouse North Carolina. The sequencing of easy and hard opponents is not the whole story, however. The Billikens' 17th game, where a win would have been expected (based on it being an odd-numbered game) and indeed occurred, was at Xavier (Ohio), who came into the game against SLU with a 12–2 record. At some point once St. Louis's alternation pattern became quite pronounced (I don't remember after exactly how many games that was), I began blogging about the repetitive win-lose cycle, providing "*n* choose *k*" results along the way. Among the outlets that took an interest was *Sports Illustrated on Campus*, which on February 6, 2006, ran an item about my calculations.[2]

Back in the early part of the 2003–2004 men's college season, basketball blogger Ken Pomeroy drew attention to Bucknell's rather volatile free-throw shooting.[3] The Bison could be down—way down—one night, but then way up another night. Specifically, November 21, 2003, at Michigan St., Bucknell went 1-for-17 from the free-throw line, only to follow that miserable effort up with perfect (9-for-9, December 3, 2003, at Northwestern) and near-perfect (14-for-15, December 6, 2003, at St. Francis of Pennsylvania) games from the stripe a short time later.

I decided to examine archived online box scores from all of Bucknell's games that season to see if the Bison continued their radical up-and-down swings on free throws or instead settled into a stable range of shooting accuracy (for two games, box scores were missing).[4] The answer, as I expected, was the latter. In 16 of the 27 Bucknell games for which data were available, the Bison's free-throw percentage was in the 60s. In fact, there were 10 games in which Bucknell's free-throw percentage fell into an even narrower range, between 63 and 67 percent. Free-throw shooting is one of the relatively few tasks in sports where the quality of the opposition should have no effect on players' ability to perform, hence performance should stabilize. A team, such as Bucknell in this case, might show some degree of wild fluctuation, but it is unlikely to continue long-term. As a little "kicker" to this story, however, the Bison did stray once more in a big way from the range into which they had stabilized, going a perfect nine-of-nine on free throws in the regular-season finale, at Colgate.

As a third bizarre basketball story, I wanted to mention an NCAA women's basketball "Sweet Sixteen" game in 2000 pitting my local team, the Texas Tech Lady Raiders, against Notre Dame. When Notre Dame, the higher seed of the two teams, jumped out to a 17–0 lead, things obviously did not look good for Texas Tech. However, in certainly one of the most unlikely developments I've ever seen, the Lady Raiders came back to score 17 straight points to tie the game. Given that two teams have each scored 17 points, there would, of course, be a huge number of ways this could happen. Team A might go ahead 2–0, Team B might bounce back for a 5–2 lead, Team A might close to within 5–4, and so forth, until the teams were tied at 17. Or Team B might lead 3–0, Team A might close to within 3–2, Team B might then expand its lead to 7–2, etc., until the teams fought to a 17-all tie. The number of ways two teams could reach a 17–17 tie would have to be staggering. And yet, arguably the strangest way of all—one team scoring 17 straight and then the other returning the favor—is what actually happened with Notre Dame and Texas Tech. By the way, Texas Tech won the game, 69–65.[5] (On January 17, 2011, in a battle of the highly ranked Pittsburgh and Syracuse men's college-basketball teams, something similar *almost* occurred. Pitt took a 19–0 lead, only to have Syracuse reel off 17 straight points to pull within 2. The Panthers scored next, though, preventing the Orange from recording its own 19–0 run to tie the game.[6])

For the final example of this brief chapter, let's turn to hockey. This example might be considered an instance of hot play by one team and cold play by the other, but I just find the whole thing odd. On April 10, 2010, the NHL's Boston Bruins found a hot scoring hand at an unusual time—while outnumbered on the ice by the opposing team! As part of a 4–2 win over the Carolina Hurricanes, Boston achieved the unprecedented feat of scoring three short-handed goals within the same penalty.[7] For readers who don't follow hockey closely, it is important to note that goals by a shorthanded team (that has lost a player due to penalty) are extremely rare. Given its precarious situation, a shorthanded team will usually be very defensive-minded, staying near the goal it is defending and hitting the puck to the other end of the rink (i.e., "icing the puck") to kill time and get a reprieve from the advantaged team's offensive attack (icing is not allowed when teams are at equal strength, but is permitted for a shorthanded team).

League statistics for the 2009–2010 season (as of April 9) showed that even the team with the most shorthanded goals, the eventual Stanley Cup champion Chicago Blackhawks, didn't have that many, totaling 13 in 81 games. The Tampa Bay Lightning had scored only two shorthanded goals in 80 games. Thus, Boston scored more shorthanded goals during a single two-minute penalty than Tampa Bay had scored all season! As documented in the play-by-play sheet, the following sequence of events took place:

The Bruins' Matt Hunwick got a two-minute hooking penalty with 18 seconds remaining in the first period. Those 18 seconds expired uneventfully, sending the teams to the locker room for a break, but Boston still had to play short-handed with Hunwick in the penalty box for the first 1:42 of the second period (unless Carolina scored, in which case Boston, as the shorthanded team, would immediately be restored to its full complement of skaters).[8]

When action resumed, however, it was Boston doing all the quick scoring, racking up goals with 0:32, 1:21, and 1:36 having elapsed in the second period. Ironically, it must have been Carolina, and not Boston, who was relieved when the Bruins' penalty ended!

IV
Two Noteworthy Athletes

14

Alex Rodriguez

Alex Rodriguez ("A-Rod") of baseball's New York Yankees—like Kobe Bryant of basketball's Los Angeles Lakers, who is featured in the next chapter—is a controversial sports icon. In common with Bryant, Rodriguez plays under the microscope of a major media market, makes an annual salary of more than $20 million, and has been involved in various scandals that are well documented elsewhere. For our purposes, the question in this chapter is whether Rodriguez is a streaky hitter.

As we analyze A-Rod's potential streakiness, we'll be drawing from chapter 2, the introduction to statistical methods. One important point to start with is that, for an athlete *really* to be streaky, he or she must exhibit spells of both hot and cold performance. Rodriguez seems to meet this criterion. In addition to his many hot streaks (described in this chapter), A-Rod can also disappear offensively, as in his 1-for-14 hitting collapse in the 2006 playoffs vs. Detroit.

However, less than a month into the next season, he had his bat going again. On April 20, 2007, Rodriguez hit two homers in a loss to the Boston Red Sox. According to a game article: "Rodriguez went 3-for-4 and joined Mike Schmidt, who hit 12 homers in the first 15 games in 1976, as the fastest to reach a dozen in baseball history."[1] Around this same time, Trent McCotter, who tracks highly specialized records, notified the SABR online discussion group that A-Rod appeared to be closing in on the mark for most consecutive games with two or more total bases offensively (e.g., two or more singles in a game, or one or more doubles, triples, or homers; walks do not count). Ultimately, Rodriguez tied Harry Heilmann's 1928 mark at 19 games (I independently verified via Retrosheet, a website on which box scores from nearly all MLB games are archived, that Rodriguez and Heilmann each achieved two or more total bases in 19 straight games). It remains possible, however, that some other player has done as well or better but has not had his feat detected.

Though there was substantial anecdotal evidence regarding A-Rod's streakiness, more systematic analyses were needed. In mid-2007, I found a spectacular visual display of A-Rod's sequences of home-run and non–home-run games, not just for 2007, but for each season of his career. Done by Ryan Armbrust at a blog called the *Pastime*, the displays (known as "sparklines") consisted of horizontal sequences of little tick-marks, each one representing a game; a grey tick-mark indicated a homerless game for A-Rod, whereas a red tick-mark indicated that Rodriguez had homered in a game (the higher the red tick-mark, the more homers he had hit in the game). Armbrust contended that A-Rod had "been a streaky home run hitter his entire career, as shown by the sparklines."[2]

However, as social psychologist David Myers noted in his book *Intuition: Its Powers and Perils*, "Random sequences seldom look random, because they contain more streaks than people expect."[3] Any interested readers can demonstrate this for themselves by following Myers's example and flipping coins for a while. Every so often, you'll get streaks of several heads or several tails in a row.

A statistical test to determine if A-Rod's sequences of games with (and without) at least one home run are more bunched into homogeneous segments (i.e., streaks) than would be expected by chance is thus warranted, and our tool is the aforementioned runs test. Armbrust's sparkline graphs made my analyses much easier than if I had to research all of A-Rod's individual games myself. I categorized each game into one of two groups, according to Rodriguez's performance: no homer (0), and one homer or more (1). Runs are uninterrupted sequences of zeroes or ones; we are thus using the term "run" in a particular statistical context and not in regard to how many "runs" a baseball team scores. The key to the runs test is that *streakiness is signified by few runs* (such as 11110000, which contains two runs), suggesting that an athlete has a penchant for staying in a given mode (success or failure). On the other hand, an *absence of streakiness is signified by many runs* in a sequence (such as 10100101, which contains seven runs). Further, for any given sequence, we can calculate how many runs would be *expected by chance.* Then, if the actual number of runs in a sequence turns out to be significantly smaller than expected, we can claim streakiness. Many (if not most) introductory statistics books provide detailed instruction on the runs test, for readers who are interested.

The table below shows the results of my application of Rodriguez's data (from the *Pastime*, except for a couple of months in 2007 that I gleaned myself) to the runs test. The online runs-test calculator mentioned in chapter 2 is limited to 80 cases of data. Accordingly, I first did hand calculations of A-Rod's actual (observed) and expected runs for both the first 80 games and all games of each season. With data from the first 80 games of a given season, I performed a formal runs test online only if the actual number of runs was below the expected value, as I wasn't interested in testing if A-Rod was ever *less* streaky than expected. Then, if it appeared that his actual number of runs for a full season might be substantially lower than the expected value, I also performed a runs test for games 81 and beyond in that season (in cases where he played 161 or 162 games in a season, I used his last 80 games, leaving out the 1 or 2 in the middle of the season). The results are charted in table 14.1.

Table 14.1 Summary of Alex Rodriguez's expected and actual numbers of homogeneous-outcome runs during particular seasons and parts of seasons (stretches with fewer actual runs than expected, shown in *italics*, suggest possible streakiness).

Year	Number of Season Games (Full = total number of games played by Rodriguez)	Number of Runs Expected by Chance	Actual Number of Runs
1996*	First 80 games Full (146 games)	31 52	35 57
1997	First 80 games Full (141 games)	21 39	21 41
1998	First 80 games Full (161 games)	34 60	37 61
1999	First 80 games Full (129 games)	34 53	39 57
2000	First 80 games Full (148 games)	*30* *56.5*	*27* *48#*
2001	First 80 games Full (162 games)	30 68	31 75
2002	First 80 games Full (162 games)	*31* *67*	*29* *65*
2003	First 80 games Full (161 games)	29 65	32 62
2004	First 80 games Full (155 games)	29 53	32 55
2005	First 80 games Full (162 games)	25 *64*	25 *63*
2006	First 80 games Full (154 games)	*28* *50.5*	*24* *49*
2007	First 80 games	*35*	*30*

* Shown on the *Pastime* website as 1995.
# For his final 68 games, Rodriguez showed statistically significant evidence of streakiness ($p = .02$).

One finding that initially jumps out at me is that A-Rod has been as (or more) likely to exhibit a *greater* number of homogeneous runs than expected by chance (the opposite of streakiness) in a season, as he has been to exhibit fewer runs. For one sizable segment of games—his final 68 of the 2000 season—Rodriguez showed pronounced streakiness, experiencing appreciably fewer stretches of home-run and non–home-run games than would be expected by chance. This sequence met the traditional criterion for statistical significance, namely that there was less than a 5 percent chance of such a result occurring just by chance. There were also three portions of seasons (the last 80 games of 2003; the first 80 games of 2006; and the first 80 games of 2007) where A-Rod nearly achieved statistically significant streakiness (the associated probability levels were equal to or slightly below 10 percent likelihood of a chance finding). Overall, therefore, I would say there is some very modest evidence of Alex Rodriguez being a streaky home-run hitter, whose dingers tend to come in bunches. But to a large extent, the bunches we see in the visual depictions tend to be the result of randomness.

Later on in the 2007 season, after I had done the runs-test analyses, Rodriguez unveiled a new batting stretch—this time of the cold variety—to further his credentials as a streaky hitter. As reported in an article on the Yankees' August 2, 2007, loss to the Chicago White Sox, A-Rod "ended a career-high hitless streak at 22 at-bats when he singled in the second" (the grey summary box above the article refers to an "0–21 skid," but I believe 22 is the correct number of at-bats).[4] His pre-slump batting average was .312 (116/372), which translates into a pre-slump failure rate of 1-.312,or .688. Raising the latter figure to the 22nd power (for 22 straight at-bats) yields a probability of .0003 (3-in-10,000) of A-Rod having such a drought.

Unfortunately for Rodriguez, he did poorly again in the 2007 playoffs. With the Yankees' elimination at the hands of Cleveland, here's an accounting of his postseason woes from an Associated Press article:

> He is mired in an 8-for-59 (.136) playoff spiral dating to his Game 4 home run against Boston in the 2004 ALCS.
>
> New York's biggest bopper is hitless in his last 18 playoff at-bats with runners in scoring position.
>
> Rodriguez hit a solo homer [in the finale of the Cleveland series] . . . ending a streak of 57 postseason at-bats without [a Run-Batted-In]. . . .
>
> Hitless in his last 27 postseason at-bats with any runners on base, A-Rod is certain to again face some criticism after his up-and-down postseason.[5]

For all of Rodriguez's postseason hitting slumps through 2007, the Yankee slugger really turned things around in 2009 in helping his team to the World Series title. In 15 Yankee postseason games in '09, A-Rod hit 5 doubles and 6 homers, batted .365, sported a .500 on-base percentage, and slugged at a clip of .808.[6] The latter statistic means that he nearly averaged a full base on all of his official at-bats.

15

Kobe Bryant

Kobe Bryant's displays of hot-shooting are plentiful. In addition to his 81-point game, which was discussed at the beginning of the book, Bryant also has the following accomplishments:

- He scored at least 50 points in each of four straight games (March 16–23, 2007). Wilt Chamberlain is the only NBA player to have put together a longer such streak, at seven, during the 1961–1962 season.[1]
- He hit an NBA single-game record nine consecutive three-pointers against Seattle (now Oklahoma City) on January 7, 2003, and his total of 12 three-pointers (out of 18 attempts) in that game was also a single-game record.[2] (Latrell Sprewell and Ben Gordon each later one-upped Bryant in a sense by going a perfect 9-for-9 on three-pointers in a game, which is the NBA record for number of threes *without a miss*; further, Bryant's record of 12 three-pointers in a game was later tied by Donyell Marshall.)[3]
- A few months after his three-point outburst vs. Seattle, Bryant hit 8 three-pointers in a half (out of 11 attempts) against Washington on March 28, 2003, a record that is now jointly held by six players.[4]

One element of the criteria for streakiness—that a player exhibit hot performances—clearly appears to be satisfied.

What about the second element, namely that the same player also experience stretches of coldness? With Bryant having played well over 1,000 professional games (including the playoffs), an off-night here or there would not be surprising. Yet, I honestly could not recall any episodes where he went into pronounced slumps. Finally, some web-searching led me to another of those online sports-discussion sites, where someone remarked upon Bryant's slow start in the 2008 Beijing Olympics. As I independently documented, Bryant

126

had indeed floundered in the Americans' initial two games, going 1-for-7 on threes vs. China and 0-for-8 on threes vs. Angola.[5]

Before Bryant, There Was Michael Jordan

Bryant is considered by many to be the successor to Michael Jordan, whose dynamic play led the Chicago Bulls to six NBA titles in the 1990s. Both players are the same height (6'6") and are/were equally comfortable shooting from outside or driving in for a monster dunk. Perhaps Jordan's most memorable night of streaky shooting came in the 1992 NBA Finals against Portland. As one article described it:

> In the first half of Game 1, a scorching-hot Michael Jordan hit his sixth 3-pointer and then looked over to the broadcast table and gave a disbelieving, palms-up shrug. As good as he was, not even Jordan could believe how hot he'd become—he had a Finals-record 35 points in the first half.[6]

On March 28, 2003, Bryant and Jordan faced each other, the latter playing for the Washington Wizards during a comeback after retiring from the Bulls. An article on that game included the following brief passage: "Asked if he felt he was passing the torch to Bryant, Jordan said, 'He definitely has a share of the torch, and there's a couple of other guys that carry it as well'."[7]

Whether Bryant's stretches of hot and (apparently less frequent) cold shooting cited above truly would translate into statistically significant findings of streakiness over his entire career is unknown. In fact, John Huizinga and Sandy Weil's study of top NBA shooters (described in chapter 5) suggests that Bryant would not qualify as a streaky shooter over the long term. In fairness to Bryant, however, one should consider the lengths to which rival NBA teams go in trying to defend him. Midway through the 2009 playoffs, *Sports Illustrated* ran a fascinating article entitled "Guarding Kobe." Houston Rocket defensive specialist Shane Battier was said to have several maneuvers up his sleeve: "He pushed Bryant left (where double-team help would be), kept him off the free throw line (so there were no easy points), contested every shot (with 'that hand-in-the-face activity' as Lakers coach Phil Jackson put it) and forced him to shoot deep, off-balance two-point jumpers." In game 1 of the L.A.-Houston playoff series, "Bryant shot 8 for 22 from the field while being guarded by Battier," although the Laker star performed better in game 2. Behind much of the opposition strategizing is an exquisite body of statistics, gathered in greater detail than ever before: "According to Synergy Sports Technology, which logs every play of every NBA game, Bryant drove right 49.01 percent of the time this season and left 50.99 percent of the time. In Synergy's finely parsed statistical analysis, he ranked in the top 20 percent of the league in (deep breath): shots off cuts, shots off screens, spot-up attempts, shots against single coverage in the post and off one-on-one isolation moves (and he's only slightly less effective in pick and rolls and transition)."[8]

Regardless of all the technical stuff, however, it's pretty safe to say that Bryant—along with Cleveland's (now Miami's, as of the 2010–2011 season) LeBron James, who once scored his team's final 25 points of the game, 29 of its last 30, in a key 2007 playoff win against Detroit—cannot be matched for their offensive explosiveness in today's NBA.[9]

V
Moving Forward in Our Understanding

16

Theories of What Helps (or Hinders) Athletes from Exhibiting Streakiness — and Why Fans Believe in It

In the previous chapters, I have largely let loose my sports fan and number-cruncher sides. In the remaining two chapters, my more traditional academic side takes center stage, as we look at theories, research, and implications (including for sports psychology practice).

The study of streakiness really encompasses two different major questions. First, what factors facilitate (or hinder) athletes in exhibiting streaky performances? Second, why do sports fans and other observers sometimes conclude that an athlete (or team) is a streaky performer or is in some kind of mental "zone," when the performance in question is completely consistent with a distribution of coin flips?

Let's address the first question—dealing with actual athletic performance—first. The overarching theoretical perspective I have espoused (chapter 3) is that streakiness will occur most readily with relatively simple motions (e.g., bowling, golf putting) that can be repeated quickly, so that motor memories of the action can be retained. Mike Stadler focuses, relatedly, on athletes' need to maintain concentration and attention in order to perform well.[1] Drawing upon the research of fellow psychologist Roy Baumeister and colleagues, Stadler notes that concentration appears to be a finite, depletable resource, where expenditure of mental energy on one task can compromise performance on an immediately following task. Writes Stadler, "As good as elite athletes are, there is likely a limit to how long they can maintain their full attention. The ups and downs of the ability to exert the will may account for the cyclic pattern of streaks and slumps."[2]

As we saw in chapter 3, researchers at Stanford found that brain mechanisms involved in planning actions are unlikely to be replicable time after time when performing a task repeatedly.[3] Even if brain processes could lead to consistency in repeating an action, however, there would still be impediments to the perfect repetition of athletic motions needed to produce widespread streaky performance.

Most Americans have probably watched the game show *The Price is Right* at least a few times (the show has been on the air every weekday for the last 38 years!). There's a game on the show called Plinko, in which contestants ascend a podium to drop a large poker-type chip down a huge inclined pegboard, with the chip bouncing off different pegs as it works its way down. At the bottom of the board are slots representing different monetary prize values, a single $10,000 slot being the best (for most of the show's history, the most valuable slot was worth $5,000) and a $0 slot being the one to avoid. The contestant can earn multiple turns at playing Plinko, depending on how many chips he or she wins in some preliminary pricing games. Just as a basketball player who had made several straight free-throws would try to release the next shot exactly as he or she had done previously, a Plinko contestant would try similarly to repeat a success (assuming he or she had multiple chips). Specifically, a player whose previous chip tumbled down into the $10,000 slot would try to release his or her next chip *exactly* as before—from the same location, at the same angle, with the same force, etc. Such an attempt to place the chip on a desired path would almost certainly be futile, however.

As one element of *chaos theory*, it is known that even the tiniest discrepancy between the conditions on the two releases—the contestant's hand position being slightly different, extra molecules of perspiration getting onto the chip, variations in the intensity of the air conditioner, etc.—would likely result in different pathways. Steven Strogatz, to whom we referred earlier as a collaborator on one of the Joe DiMaggio computer-simulation studies, wrote in his 2003 book *Sync* about a spinning object called a waterwheel, which is divided into many small chambers. When propped up at an angle and rotating so that water from an adjoining reservoir can enter or exit its chambers, the wheel will careen from spinning clockwise to counter-clockwise, unpredictably. Notes Strogatz:

> What's even more disconcerting is that the behavior is not reproducible. The next time you turn on the waterwheel, its patterns of reversals will be different. If you take tremendous care to ensure that everything is almost the same as it was the last time, its motion will track for a while but then diverge, yielding a completely unrelated sequence of turns and reversals thereafter.
>
> Of course, if you started the wheel absolutely the same way, it would repeat. . . . But in the real world . . . the variables are never exactly the

same from run to run. The slightest difference—a drop of water in one of the chambers, left over from the previous experiment, or a puff of air exhaled by an overexcited spectator—will alter the motion of the wheel, at first imperceptibly, but very soon with incalculable consequences.[4]

In short, neither a Plinko chip nor a basketball shot will necessarily travel the same way on two successive trials, despite the player's best attempts to release the object as consistently as possible once he or she has encountered success.

On other types of tasks, it may be best for athletes to try to execute their skills in a largely spontaneous manner, without obsessing about executing the maneuver exactly the same way as before. In some situations, excessive thought can be harmful. Psychologist Sian Beilock provided the following quote to a golf publication:

> Pressure causes worries about the performance and its outcomes. . . . For skills that run largely outside of working memory—for example, the easy three-foot putt to win the tourney—these worries seem to cause people to try and control or monitor their performance in a manner that disrupts the automated or proceduralized processes of execution that are normally not attended to.[5]

As discussed in chapter 10, free-throw shooting—an activity where the game is stopped and a player can attempt a shot undisturbed, at his or her own pace—appears to have a "ceiling" at around 70–75 percent success that the average player has not been able to exceed. Considering all the seemingly complex factors related to athletes' mental states and the physics at small scales, it is no wonder that players who shoot well above 75 percent and go on hot streaks from the free-throw line are quite rare. In the past few NBA regular seasons, less than 10 percent of the league's roughly 360 players exceeded 85 percent accuracy.[6]

In addition to theories of factors that may help or hinder athletes in exhibiting streaky performance, academics have also offered suggestions of why sports observers often over-interpret athletes' runs of success and failure as something meaningful (e.g., "She's a streaky shooter," "He can get in the zone") when they may just be the product of randomness. The first theory I'll discuss holds that we can be locked into thinking that however a situation is now, it will continue to be the same well on into the future. This idea comes from the book *Stumbling on Happiness* by psychologist Daniel Gilbert. The premise of the book is that we tend not to be very good at predicting how we would react

emotionally, if a given event were to occur in the future. For example, if someone were asked to predict how he or she would feel if a favorite sports team
were to win a championship, the person's estimate of future happiness would
likely exceed his or her actual happiness if the team actually won a championship (and you could survey the fan at that later time). Gilbert and his colleague Tim Wilson refer to this area of research as "affective forecasting."

I did not start reading the book with hot hand research in mind. However,
Gilbert's chapter on "presentism" (expecting present conditions to last indef-
initely) really seemed to fit what may be going on with hot hand perceptions.
The meaning of presentism can be grasped via a couple of Gilbert quotes:
"When brains plug holes in their conceptualizations of yesterday and tomor-
row, they tend to use a material called today."[7] "If the present lightly colors our
remembered pasts, it thoroughly infuses our imagined futures."[8]

To use basketball as an illustration, presentism can be applied to hot hand
perceptions as follows. An observer sees a player make several shots in a row
(present) and naturally expects a high likelihood of the player making his or
her next several shots (future). Such expectations presumably would be what
give rise to the thinking that a team should always pass the ball to a hot shooter.
As discussed in chapter 5, however, Jay Koehler and Caryn Conley found that
players' shooting percentages immediately following TV announcers' hot hand
exclamations (e.g., "Legler is on fire") during NBA three-point shooting contests were no different than their overall baseline shooting percentages, thus
showing once again that the present was not predictive of the future.[9]

In a very different context, Richard Posner's book analyzing the 2008 economic crisis made a number of points that reminded me of Gilbert's concept
of presentism. One of the widely identified culprits for the economic collapse
is, of course, the housing bubble in the immediately preceding years;
Wikipedia defines such a bubble as, "rapid increases in valuations of real prop-
erty such as housing until they reach unsustainable levels relative to incomes
and other economic elements."[10] As Posner discusses, during a housing bubble
people think (presently high) prices will continue to rise, whereas during a de-
flationary period, they'll hoard money, thinking (presently low) prices will
continue to go down.[11]

The second theory for why fans of elite sports (in golf, at least) may read
too much into a player's streak of a few successes or failures draws upon what
social psychologists call the *false consensus* effect.[12] If an individual has some attribute (personality trait, opinion, etc.), he or she will often think the attribute
in question is fairly widespread in the population—more widespread, in fact,

than it actually is. It will be recalled from chapter 7 that Cotton and Price found those between 12 and 17 years of age to exhibit significant streakiness in golf; by extension, one might also expect novice adults to show streaky performance. Cotton and Price put all this information together in suggesting that layperson golfers (who do tend to be streaky) may, via the false consensus effect, come to believe that streakiness is a widespread characteristic of golfers, including professionals. As these authors state, "If people recognize that they (or other amateurs) experience the hot hand when participating in an activity, then they may overestimate the likelihood that others also experience the hot hand."[13]

The third theory, from anthropologists Andreas Wilke and H. Clark Barrett, suggests that it may be in our evolutionary heritage to have looked for survival-relevant objects to be distributed in streak-like clumps: "In nature, clumps are the norm rather than the exception in diverse natural phenomena including the distributions of animals, plants, minerals, water, human settlements, and weather."[14] Thus, regarding our mental processing of information, "The existence of one or more decision-making adaptations to exploit such clumps might be expected on evolutionary grounds."[15] These authors propose further that "we possess an evolved foraging system that is designed to help us locate and make decisions about clumped resources, but we do *not* possess an evolved system designed to help us think about truly random ones."[16]

Wilke and Barrett conducted simulation experiments in which participants were asked to work through sequences of trials, where a key outcome would be present or absent on one trial (on a random basis), and predict whether the outcome would be present on the next trial. Some of the sequences were meant to resemble nature (e.g., photographs of seemingly adjacent trees that each would either have a bird's nest or not), whereas others were not (e.g., coin tosses). Participants came from two distinct populations: students at a major U.S. university, and a small, rural "hunter-horticulturalist" community in South America. The main finding was that, across populations and task types, participants tended to view objects with a "hot hand" mindset, that whatever the result was on one trial, it would be the same on the next trial. There were two exceptions, however. The college students saw the outcomes of coin tosses (and also whether places along a city street would have bus stops) in random terms. This study thus suggests that seeing objects in clumps is a pronounced mental pattern (what Wilke and Barrett call a "psychological default"), which for the most part, can only be overridden by experience with sequences that are known to be blatantly random (i.e., the occurrences of heads and tails on coin tosses).

Writing in the *New York Times* about athletic skids, quantitative analyst Ian Ayres wondered, essentially, how long of a drought members of the sports media would need to see from a player before pronouncing him or her to be in a slump. Wrote Ayres, "It might be fun to do a study to [figure] out the implicit level of statistical significance that reporters require before they use 'slump' or 'drought.' I'd predict that this implicit level varies with how much they like the athlete—so that they would start using the term more quickly with regard to [Alex] Rodriguez than, say, [Derek] Jeter."[17] The research of Wilke and Barrett suggests that sports reporters and announcers would need minimal evidence to jump to such a conclusion.

To end this chapter, it seems appropriate to quote, once again, the late Harvard scholar Stephen Jay Gould:

> We believe in "hot hands" because we must impart meaning to a pattern—and we like meanings that tell stories about heroism, valor, and excellence. We believe that long streaks and slumps must have direct causes internal to the sequence itself, and we have no feel for the frequency and length of sequences in random data.[18]

17

Conclusions

Teams and individual athletes go on streaks. In fact, I've tried to share what I think are some of the most interesting and impressive ones I'm aware of. What I also hope to have instilled with this book is that many streaks do not exceed—in their magnitude or frequency—what would be expected based on coin-tossing. They're just chance occurrences. Other streaks, however, such as Joe DiMaggio's hitting in 56 consecutive games, really do appear to transcend random processes, but these kinds of streaks are very rare.

Some sports fans may look at findings of a substantial chance component in athletic performances and ask whether the statisticians are trying to take the humanity out of sport, reduce sports to numbers, or claim player abilities don't matter. Far from it! We all know that there is plenty of humanity in sports, based on totally unexpected meltdowns from star players, or heroic actions from relatively unknown athletes. Further, abilities matter a lot. A basketball player with, say, a 40 percent season-long shooting percentage is going to get you a lot more points than one with a 30 percent hit rate (provided they take the same number of shots). Teams should thus try to get players with the highest overall success rates possible (e.g., shooting percentages, batting averages), without worrying about whether those players are "streaky."

A classic example of this would be former University of Texas softball pitcher Cat Osterman, who threw 20 no-hitters in her collegiate career.[1] This accomplishment is unquestionably impressive. However, the infrequency with which she gave up hits in general (her career opponents' batting average was .095; 343 hits allowed in 3,601 official at-bats)[2] and the seven-inning length of softball games suggest that Osterman should have recorded a fair number of no-hitters. The probability of her recording an out on any given official at-bat would be an estimated 1 − .095, or .905 (this calculation makes the

137

simplifying assumption that all batters she faced were equally good hitters, thus the use of the same hit/out percentage for each). Then, to estimate Osterman's probability of retiring the opposing batters on all 21 of their official at-bats in a game, we take $(.905)^{21}$, which yields .123. (Walks, hit batters, etc., are excluded, as we're focusing on no-hitters rather than perfect games.) Osterman, in fact, threw no-hitters .136 of the time (20 in her 147 career starts). Thus, the proportion of games in which she threw no-hitters closely matched the proportion that would be expected based on overall averages. The bottom line is that Cat Osterman is a pitcher you'd want on your softball team, even if she isn't technically "streaky" in the sense discussed above.

IMPLICATIONS FOR SPORT
PSYCHOLOGY PRACTICE

Much of the research reviewed in this book suggests that athletes' performances on a week-to-week or month-to-month—if not game-to-game—basis generally fall in line with what would be expected from their longer-term records of success and failure. That does *not* mean, however, that coaches, sport psychologists, and teaching professionals cannot provide meaningful input to help their clients perform better. Russell Clark, whose golf studies we read about in chapter 7, offered some implications of his research for sport psychology practice, during a 2004 online chat he held in conjunction with my Hot Hand website:

> Since the data on hole-to-hole scores strongly suggest that past performance is not a good predictor of future behavior, my recommendation to PGA Teaching professionals and sports psychologists is rather simple. . . . If [after verifying the lack of streakiness in the client's scores] these outcomes hold true, and I believe they will for most players, it should make it easier for the player to concentrate on each shot without dwelling on previous failures or having excessive concern with the next. Then, the task becomes how best to execute the next shot. Once one realizes the effects of the past have been grossly exaggerated, the teaching professional and sports psychologist can assist the golfer in developing and maintaining a well-defined pre-shot routine and teach a variety of techniques for regulation of arousal. And don't forget the need for the constant honing of skills and even the learning of new skills. . . . For the highly skilled golfer, one simple truth should constantly be emphasized. The player is going to have . . . far more good holes than bad holes.

Knowing this, plus the fact the bad holes are not likely to be followed by bad holes, should enable the person to expect superior, or at least good, performance on each shot.

In very much the same vein, Rosabeth Moss Kanter's book *Confidence* details some of the philosophies of "Coach K," the legendary leader of Duke University men's basketball:

Confidence motivates people to put in extra effort, to stretch beyond their previous limits, to rebound from setbacks, or to play through injuries anyway. People with confidence stay in the game no matter what. Duke's Mike Krzyzewski called this the principle of "next play." "Don't take what you did in this play to the next play—positive or negative," he told us.[3]

Finally, Mike Stadler discusses how "Sports psychologists try to help athletes stem the ebb and flow of concentration and focus," but also focus on the next play.[4] In formulating this advice, Stadler draws upon the suggestions of sports scientists and psychologists who have worked with MLB teams. There thus seems to be a consensus among coaches and academic researchers that athletes should focus on the next shot, pitch, possession, etc., and not dwell on the past. Playing with confidence and sustained attention also appear to be important.

FINAL THOUGHTS

I have been fascinated by the hot-hand controversy since I first heard of this line of research on August 24, 1985. On that day, I attended a talk at the annual American Psychological Association convention by Amos Tversky, entitled "Misconceptions of Chance Processes in Basketball," the findings of which also appeared in the famous Gilovich, Vallone, and Tversky article cited multiple times in this book. Throughout the rest of the 1980s and into the early 1990s, when there was no World Wide Web to allow instant communications within large, virtual town-hall discussion groups, my interest in the hot hand waned. But by the late 1990s, I realized I could conduct my own hot-hand analyses and e-mail them to large groups of colleagues via electronic interest groups ("listserves") organized around professional academic societies. From there, I went on to create the original Hot Hand website in 2002, which I then converted into blog format in 2006 (http://thehothand.blogspot.com). Now, not a day goes by when I'm not watching sporting events and checking the news to learn of any new sports streaks that I can write about on my blog.

I (and other scholars) have come across two camps of people—sports fans who believe in streakiness and are thus highly resistant to the idea that athletes' runs of success are just like rare streaks of several consecutive heads or tails in coin-tossing, and statisticians who, for the most part, readily accept this idea. With this book, I have attempted to bridge the gap, arguing for streakiness where I think the evidence supports it, and for its absence where I think the studies are extensive and large enough to cast doubt on the phenomenon. Whether I've convinced hardcore believers on either side, I don't know. Still, if this book leads sports fans to view games through more of a statistical lens than they had before, to shout "What are the odds?" at their television sets when they see something unusual, to consider seriously the role of chance as an explanation for what they're seeing, and to view isolated sports occurrences in the larger context of all the games that have taken place and all the players who have walked into the athletic arena, then I will be happy.

NOTES

Chapter 1. Introduction

1. Lewis, *Moneyball*, 244.
2. Sports Illustrated (SI) Vault, "Micheal Williams streak."
3. Elias Sports Bureau, "Elias Says."
4. Wikipedia, "MLB Consecutive Games Played Streaks."
5. Wikipedia, "Longest NCAA Division I Football Winning Streaks."
6. Moran, "Leinert Carries Southern Cal."
7. Gould, "The Streak of Streaks."
8. Battista, "Saying He Won't."
9. Kanter, *Confidence.*

Chapter 2. Statistical Methods

1. Gilovich, Vallone, and Tversky, "Hot Hand in Basketball."
2. King and Minium, *Statistical Reasoning*, 169.
3. Warrack, "The Great Streak."
4. Ibid., 43 (box).
5. Hurvich, "Winning and Losing Streaks."
6. Albert and Bennett, *Curve Ball*, 144.
7. King and Minium, *Statistical Reasoning.*
8. Diaconis and Mosteller, "Methods for Studying Coincidences."
9. Pomeroy, "Move the Line Back."

Chapter 3. Evidence Supportive of a Hot Hand

1. Abbott, "Hot and Heavy."

2. Bowling Digital, "Dorin-Ballard Almost."

3. Dorsey-Palmateer and Smith, "Bowlers' Hot Hands."

4. Ibid., 38.

5. Smith, "Horseshoe Pitchers."

6. Gilden and Gray Wilson, "Streaks in Skilled Performance," 261.

7. Ibid., 263.

8. Klaassen and Magnus, "Are Points in Tennis," 505.

9. Reifman, analysis of NHL hardest shot contest.

10. Orenstein, "On the Golf Tee."

11. McCotter, "Hitting Streaks Don't."

12. Paulos, "Does Joe DiMaggio's."

13. McCotter, 68.

14. Ibid., 69.

Chapter 4. "We Are a Team of Runs"

1. Bedore, "A Big, Easy Blowout."

2. See Dean Oliver's 2004 book *Basketball on Paper* for further discussion of offensive efficiency.

Chapter 5. Evidence Against a Hot Hand: Basketball

1. Associated Press, "Texas Tech Upsets K-State."

2. Gilovich, Vallone, and Tversky, "Hot Hand in Basketball," 297.

3. Dorsey-Palmateer and Smith, "Bowlers' Hot Hands."

4. Ian Ayres published a wonderful book in 2007 called *Super Crunchers*, which details the increasing role of huge databases in many areas of life, such as business marketing and government policymaking.

5. Huizinga and Weil, "Hot Hand."

6. Abbott, "Hot and Heavy."

7. Huizinga and Weil, "Hot Hand," 12.

8. Ibid., 29.

9. Burns, "Heuristics as Beliefs."

10. Ibid., 317.

11. Koehler and Conley, "The Hot Hand Myth."

12. Buckeye Commentary, "Basketball."

Chapter 6. Evidence Against a Hot Hand: Baseball

1. Albright, "A Statistical Analysis."

2. Levitt and Dubner, *Freakonomics*, 162.

3. Albright, "A Statistical Analysis," 1182.

4. Albert and Bennett, *Curve Ball*.

5. Singer, "For Derby."

6. Ibid., 345.

7. Albert, "Streaky Hitting."

8. Ibid., 28.

9. Cerrone, "Stats: David Wright."

10. Tango, Lichtman, and Dolphin, *The Book*.

11. Cameron, "Projecting Future Performance."

12. James, "Evidence of Non-Random Clusters."

13. Albert and Bennett, *Curve Ball*.

14. Studeman, "Ten Things."

15. Henderson and Hooper, "When Lady Luck."

16. Spencer, quote on Fox 34 News.

17. James, "Underestimating the Fog."

18. UCLA Academic Technology Services, "Statistical Computing Seminars."

19. Bar-Eli, Avugos, and Raab, "Twenty Years"; Oskarsson, Van Boven, McClelland, and Hastie, "What's Next?"

20. Sela and Simonoff, "Does Momentum Exist?"

21. Ibid., 151.

Chapter 7. Revisiting Golf (Briefly)

1. Clark, "An Examination."

2. Clark, "An Analysis," 366.

3. Ibid., 371.

4. Livingston, "The Hot Hand," 7.

5. Ibid, 4–5.

6. Cotton and Price, "The Hot Hand," 2–3.

7. Ibid., 8.

Chapter 8. Joe DiMaggio

1. Baseball Reference website, Joe DiMaggio's 1941 batting gamelog.

2. Wikipedia, "Joe DiMaggio."

3. Gould, "The Streak of Streaks."

4. Lackritz, "Two of Baseball's," 17.

5. D'Aniello, "DiMaggio's Hitting Streak," 34.

6. Stephens, "Wittels Two Shy."

7. FIUsports.com, baseball season statistics.

8. Associated Press, "Garrett Wittels' Hitting Streak Ends."

9. Brown and Goodrich, "Calculating the Odds."

10. Ibid., 40.

11. Arbesman and Strogatz, "A Journey."

12. Ibid.

13. Ibid.

14. Ibid.

15. Ibid.

16. Rockoff and Yates, "Chasing DiMaggio."

17. Ibid.

18. Chance, "What Are the Odds?"

19. Ibid., 39.

20. Winston, *Mathletics*.

21. McCotter, "DiMaggio's Challengers"; McCotter, "More on Streaks."

22. McCotter, "More on Streaks," 44.

23. McCotter, "Hitting Streaks."

24. Associated Press, "DeRosa's Third."

25. Associated Press, "Report: Guerrero Signs."

Chapter 9. *Really* **Hot Teams**

1. Hein, "UCLA's 88-game."

2. Rosen, *The Pivotal Season*, 97.

3. Basketball Reference, "1971–72 Los Angeles Lakers."

4. Boston Celtics webpage. "Making the Schedule."

5. Simmons, *The Book of Basketball.*

6. Farkas, "Comparing Win/Loss."

7. Fleder, *The College Football Book.*

8. Lewis, *Moneyball.*

9. Neyer, "Figuring Out the Laws."

10. Neyer, "Figuring Out the A's."

11. Feller, *An Introduction.* (See pages 324–25 for relevant formulas; later elaboration by commentators are at http://mathforum.org/library/drmath/view/56637.html.)

12. Astros Baseball Talk, "100 Win Teams."

13. Albert, "Streakiness in Team," 43.

14. A transcript of Albert and Bennett's answers to questions from me and readers of my Hot Hand website is no longer available online, but is available upon request to alan.reifman@ttu.edu.

15. Singer, "Phillies' Comeback."

16. Ibid., 417.

17. Ibid., 415.

18. Ibid., 416.

19. Ibid., 418.

20. Ibid., 419.

21. Currie, "Ball from Cubs' Playoff Loss."

22. Garber, "Trinity Squash."

23. Conyers, "Trinity Captures 12th."

24. Trinity Athletics, "Trinity Men's Squash."

25. Altavilla, "Complete Transcript."

26. Associated Press, "Jeanette Pohlen, Cardinal End."

27. Associated Press, "Villanova Halts UConn's 70-Game Streak."

28. Associated Press, "Penn State's Win Streak."

29. Timmermann, "Perfection Is Open."

30. Steiner, *Group Processes.*

Chapter 10. Hot Basketball Shooting

1. Branch, "For Free Throws."

2. Ibid.

3. Associated Press, "Deacons Aided."

4. Associated Press, "Wake Misses."

5. Pomeroy, "Move the Line Back."

6. Associated Press, "Mavericks' Rally."

7. ESPN Sports Century, "April Classic Moments."

8. Douchant, "Greatest 63 Games."

9. Wolff, "The Man Couldn't Miss."

10. White, "Nearly Perfect."

11. Hartwig, "A Tool."

12. D3Hoops, "Lincoln Pours."

13. Santoliquito, "Lincoln Sets."

14. Shouler, "Zoning In," 188.

15. Ibid., 195.

16. Associated Press, "Complete Domination."

17. Costandi, "Kicking Performance."

18. NBA.com, Derek Fisher.

19. Aroune, "Beyond Rudy."

20. Associated Press, "No. 4 Wazzu."

21. Associated Press, "Iowa's Barrage."

Chapter 11. Hot Hands in Other Sports

1. Associated Press, "A Scoreless Streak."

2. Keri, "Forty Years Later."

3. Deane, "Gibson Was Great."

4. Crasnick, "Baseball's Law."

5. Bush, "Dick Dietz."

6. Fischer et al., *Inequality by Design*, 130, "Baseball: How Rules Help Pick the Winners."

7. Associated Press, "Buehrle Sets."

8. Associated Press, "Backe, Astros Avoid Three-Game Sweep."

9. Manuel, "Making Sense."

10. MLB.com, "Four Straight."

11. Gamecock Athletics, "Carolina Opens."

12. Babineck, "Vanderjagt Sets Record."

13. Associated Press, "Titans Narrowly Hold Off Texans' Rally."

14. Kelley, "Most Consecutive Wins."

15. Wikipedia, "Byron Nelson."

16. Kelley, "Byron Nelson's 1945 Tournament Results."

17. Gonzales, "'Regular Guy'."

18. Associated Press, "Selanne Scores Twice."

19. Ibid.

20. The Goaltender Home Page (hockeygoalies.org).

21. Peters, "Giguere, Mighty Ducks."

22. Lyman, "On Chess."

Chapter 12: Cold Streaks

1. Biglin, "On Soccer."

2. Kanter, *Confidence*, 121–22.

3. Chen and Robinson, "Flashback."

4. Sexton, "Don't Pin This Loss on Young."

5. Frey, "For Young, Three Hits."

6. DaytonFlyers.com, "Johnson's Free Throws."

7. NCAA, 2008–2009 men's basketball records.

8. Associated Press, "OSU Women's Basketball."

9. Associated Press, "Indiana's Davis Notches First Win."

10. Wikipedia, "United States Triple Crown."

Chapter 13: Unusual Streaks (Neither Hot nor Cold)

1. ESPN.com, Saint Louis Billikens.

2. *Sports Illustrated on Campus*, "Hot or Not."

3. Pomeroy, "Bucking the Trend."

4. ESPN.com, Bucknell Bison.

5. *New York Times*, NCAA Tournament: Women.

6. Associated Press, "Fourth-ranked Pittsburgh."

7. Associated Press, "Bruins Score 3 Short-Handed Goals."

8. ESPN.com, Hurricanes-Bruins play-by-play sheet.

Chapter 14. Alex Rodriguez

1. Associated Press, "Red Sox Rally."

2. Armbrust, "A-Rod's Home Runs."

3. Myers, *Intuition*, 134.

4. Associated Press, "Yankees, White Sox."

5. Associated Press, "Rodriguez Homers."

6. Deadspin.com, "The Pop-psychologizing."

Chapter 15. Kobe Bryant

1. Associated Press, "Kobe Scores 50."

2. LakerStats.com, "Great Moments."

3. Wikipedia, "NBA Records."

4. Associated Press, "Kobe Dazzles."

5. International Basketball Federation, Kobe Bryant.

6. Hollinger, "Ranking the Greatest."

7. Associated Press, "Kobe Dazzles."

8. Ballard, "Guarding Kobe."

9. Associated Press, "LeBron Bewilders."

Chapter 16. Theories of What Helps (or Hinders) Athletes from Exhibiting Streakiness—and Why Fans Believe in It

1. Stadler, *Psychology of Baseball.*

2. Ibid., 154.

3. Orenstein, "On the Golf Tee."

4. Strogatz, *Sync*, 187–88.

5. Christianson, "University of Chicago."

6. Statistics for different years can be found at http://espn.go.com/nba/statistics.

7. Gilbert, *Stumbling on Happiness*, 125.

8. Ibid., 127.

9. Koehler and Conley, "The Hot Hand Myth."

10. Wikipedia, "Housing Bubble."

11. Posner, *A Failure*.

12. Ross, Greene, and House, "The False Consensus."

13. Cotton and Price, "The Hot Hand," 12.

14. Wilke and Barrett, "The Hot Hand," 162.

15. Ibid., 163.

16. Ibid.

17. Ayres, "Statistical Slumps."

18. Gould, "The Streak of Streaks."

Chapter 17. Conclusions

1. CatOsterman.com, biography.

2. TexasSports.com, University of Texas.

3. Kanter, *Confidence*, 351.

4. Stadler, *Psychology of Baseball*, 154.

BIBLIOGRAPHY

Abbott, Henry. "Hot and Heavy: About NBA Shooting." ESPN.com, April 17, 2009. http://espn.go.com/blog/truehoop/post/_/id/6241/hot-and-heavy-about -nba-shooting.

Albert, Jim. "Streakiness in Team Performance." *Chance* 17 (2004): 37–43.

———. "Streaky Hitting in Baseball." *Journal of Quantitative Analysis in Sports* 4, no. 1 (2008). http://www.bepress.com/jqas/vol4/iss1/3.

——— and Jay Bennett. *Curve Ball: Baseball, Statistics, and the Role of Chance in the Game.* New York: Copernicus, 2001.

Albright, S. Christian. "A Statistical Analysis of Hitting Streaks in Baseball." *Journal of the American Statistical Association* 88 (1993): 1175–83.

Altavilla, John. "Complete Transcript of President Obama's Comments to UConn." *Hartford Courant* (May 18, 2010). http://blogs.courant.com/uconn_womens_basketball/2010/05/complete -transcript-of-preside.html.

Arbesman, Samuel, and Steve Strogatz. "A Journey to Baseball's Alternate Universe." *New York Times* (March 30, 2008). http://www.nytimes.com/2008/03/30/opinion/30strogatz.html.

Armbrust, Ryan. "A-Rod's Home Runs, Sparkline Style." The Pastime, April 22, 2007. http://thepastime.net/2007/04/22/a-rods-home-runs-sparkline-style.

Aroune, Jim. "Beyond Rudy: Athena Senior Inspires." *Your News Now*, February 17, 2006. http://rochester.ynn.com/content/top_stories/?RegionCookie=2134 &ArId=335044.

Associated Press. "A Scoreless Streak Continues for Webb." *New York Times*, August 18, 2007. http://www.nytimes.com/2007/08/18/sports/baseball/18base.html.

————. "Backe, Astros Avoid Three-Game Sweep to Rangers." ESPN.com, May 18, 2008. http://sports.espn.go.com/mlb/recap?gameId=280518113.

————. "Bruins Score 3 Short-Handed Goals in 64 Seconds, Clinch Playoff Berth." ESPN.com, April 10, 2010. http://sports.espn.go.com/nhl/recap?gameId=300410001.

————. "Buehrle Sets Major League Record, but Takes Loss When Twins Rally." ESPN.com, July 28, 2009. http://espn.go.com/mlb/recap?gameId=290728109.

————. "Complete Domination: Lakers Rout Spurs to Finish Off Sweep." *Sports Illustrated (Online)*, May 27, 2001. http://sportsillustrated.cnn.com/basketball/nba/2001/playoffs/news/2001/05/27/spurs_lakers_ap/.

————. "Deacons Aided by Going 32-for-32 from Line." ESPN.com, January 15, 2005. http://espn.go.com/ncb/recap?gameId=250150154.

————. "DeRosa's Third Career Slam Helps Rangers Reel in Angels." ESPN.com, August 4, 2006. http://sports.espn.go.com/mlb/recap?gameId=260804103.

————. "Fourth-ranked Pittsburgh Jumps Out Early, Outlasts No. 3 Syracuse." ESPN.com, January 17, 2011. http://espn.go.com/ncb/recap?gameId=310170221.

————. "Garrett Wittels' Hitting Streak Ends" ESPN.com, February 19, 2011. http://sports.espn.go.com/ncaa/news/story?id=6137761.

————. "Indiana's Davis Notches First Win Against Kentucky." ESPN.com, December 10, 2005. http://sports.espn.go.com/ncb/recap?gameId=253440096.

————. "Iowa's Barrage of 3s Comes Too Late in Loss to No. 12 Indiana." ESPN.com, January 2, 2008. http://sports.espn.go.com/ncb/recap?gameId=280022294.

————. "Jeanette Pohlen, Cardinal End Huskies' 90-Game Winning Streak." ESPN.com, December 30, 2010. http://sports.espn.go.com/ncw/recap?gameId=303640024.

————. "Kobe Dazzles Wizards in Final Meeting with MJ." ESPN.com, March 28, 2003. http://sports.espn.go.com/nba/recap?gameId=230328013.

————. "Kobe Scores 50 (Again), Leads Lakers Past Hornets." ESPN.com, March 23, 2007. http://sports.espn.go.com/nba/recap?gameId=270323003.

————. "LeBron Bewilders Pistons as Cavaliers Inch Closer to NBA Finals." ESPN.com, May 31, 2007. http://sports.espn.go.com/nba/recap?gameId =270531008.

————. "Mavericks' Rally Based on 49 Straight Free Throws." ESPN.com, May 19, 2003. http://espn.go.com/nba/recap/_/id/230519024/dallas-mavericks-vs -san-antonio-spurs.

————. "No. 4 Wazzu Can't Stop Love, UCLA as Perfect Start Ends." ESPN.com, January 12, 2008. http://sports.espn.go.com/ncb/recap?gameId=280120026.

————. "OSU Women's Basketball: Seals' Double-Double Lifts Tech Past Oklahoma St." ESPN.com, February 21, 2009. http://newsok.com/article/3347773.

————. "Penn State's Win Streak Ends at 109." ESPN.com, September 11, 2010. http://sports.espn.go.com/ncaa/news/story?id=5562162.

————. "Red Sox Rally for Five in Eighth to Stun Yankees." ESPN.com, April 20, 2007. http://sports.espn.go.com/mlb/recap?gameId=270420102.

————. "Report: Guerrero Signs with Rangers." FoxSports.com, January 10, 2010. http://msn.foxsports.com/mlb/story/vladimir-guerrero-inks-deal-with-texas-rangers.

————. "Rodriguez Homers as Yankees Fall to Cleveland." WSVN.com, October 9, 2007. http://www.wsvn.com/news/articles/sports/MI64165/.

————. "Selanne Scores Twice but Canucks End Ducks' Win Streak in 13th Round of SO." ESPN.com, October 31, 2008. http://sports.espn.go.com/nhl/recap?gameId =281031025.

————. "Texas Tech Upsets K-State to Give Knight First Win as Head Coach." ESPN.com, February 13, 2008. http://scores.espn.go.com/ncb/recap?gameId =280442641.

————. "Titans Narrowly Hold Off Texans' Rally with Bironas' Record 8th FG." ESPN.com, October 21, 2007. http://sports.espn.go.com/nfl/recap?gameId =271021034.

————. "Villanova Halts UConn's 70-Game Streak, Wins Big East." *Sports Illustrated (Online),* March 11, 2003. http://sportsillustrated.cnn.com/basketball /college/women/news/2003/03/11/nova_uconn_ap/index.html.

————. "Wake Misses Win When Free Throw Streak Ends." ESPN.com, January 18, 2005. http://espn.go.com/ncb/recap?gameId=250180052.

———. "Yankees, White Sox Combine for 16-Run Second Inning." ESPN.com, August 2, 2007. http://sports.espn.go.com/mlb/recap?gameId=270802110.

Astros Baseball Talk. "100 Win Teams Since 1978 (Past 30 Seasons)." *Comment*, August 5, 2008. http://evilwontwin.yuku.com/topic/14144.

Ayres, Ian. "Statistical Slumps." *New York Times*, August 26, 2009. http://freakonomics.blogs.nytimes.com/2009/08/26/statistical-slumps/.

———. *Super Crunchers: Why Thinking-by-Numbers Is the New Way to Be Smart.* New York: Random House, 2007.

Babineck, Mark. "Vanderjagt Sets Record, by Kicking Colts to AFC South Crown." *USA Today*, December 28, 2003. http://www.usatoday.com/sports/football /games/2003-12-28-colts-texans_x.htm.

Ballard, Chris. "Guarding Kobe: The Greatest Testament to the Lakers' Star's Offensive Brilliance Might Be the Lengths to Which Rockets Defensive Specialist Shane Battier Will Go to Stop Him." *Sports Illustrated (SI) Vault*, May 18, 2009. http://sportsillustrated.cnn.com/vault/article/magazine/MAG1155388.

Bar-Eli, Michael, Simcha Avugos, and Markus Raab. "Twenty Years of 'Hot Hand' Research: Review and Critique." *Psychology of Sport and Exercise* 7 (2006): 525–53.

Baseball Reference. Joe DiMaggio's 1941 batting gamelog. http://www.baseball -reference.com/players/gl.cgi?n1=dimagjo01&t=b&year=1941

———. "1971-72 Los Angeles Lakers Schedule and Results." http://www.basketball-reference.com/teams/LAL/1972_games.html.

Battista, Judy. "Saying He Won't Coach, Parcells Joins Dolphins." *New York Times*, December 21, 2007. http://www.nytimes.com/2007/12/21/sports/football /21nfl.html.

Bedore, Gary. "A Big, Easy Blowout: Kansas Routs Eagles to Roll into Finals." *KU Sports (Lawrence Journal-World & 6 News Lawrence)*, April 6, 2003. http://www2.kusports.com/news/2003/apr/06/a_big_easy.

Bialik, Carl. "The Numbers Guy: A Closer Look at Sports Miracles." *Wall Street Journal Online*, September 28, 2006. http://online.wsj.com/public/article_print /SB115937351810875587-9LqLDP1JjECpTvNkOCfGVIQF5Ts_20061028.html.

Biglin, Mike. "On Soccer: Relegation: The Great Equalizer." *Milford Daily News*, May 19, 2007. http://www.milforddailynews.com/sports/x567832941.

Boston Celtics. "Making the Schedule." *Inside the Front Office*, October 20, 2008. http://www.nba.com/celtics/inside_front_office/zarren102008-trades.html.

Bowling Digital. "Dorin-Ballard Almost a '10' in PBA Women's Series Showdown Win," April 13, 2009. http://www.bowlingdigital.com/bowl/node/6350.

Branch, John. "For Free Throws, 50 Years of Practice is No Help. *New York Times*, March 3, 2009. http://www.nytimes.com/2009/03/04/sports/basketball /04freethrow.html.

Brown, Bob, and Peter Goodrich. "Calculating the Odds: DiMaggio's 56-Game Hitting Streak." *Baseball Research Journal* 32 (2003): 35–40.

Buckeye Commentary. "Basketball: Focusing on the Three," March 9, 2006. http://www.buckeyecommentary.com/oldschool/files /043740ef1a2ce643e6c36e4daabc81e1-468.html.

Burns, Bruce D. "Heuristics as Beliefs and as Behaviors: The Adaptiveness of the 'Hot Hand.'" *Cognitive Psychology* 48 (2004): 295–311.

Bush, David. "Dick Dietz: 1941-2005, 'Mule' Starred with '70 Giants." *San Francisco Chronicle*, June 30, 2005. http://www.sfgate.com/cgi-bin/article.cgi?f =/chronicle/archive/2005/06/30/SPGIBDH1LQ1.DTL.

Cameron, Dave. "Projecting Future Performance." U.S.S. Mariner: Seattle Mariner and Baseball Analysis, August 20, 2007. http://ussmariner.com/2007/08/20 /projecting-future-performance.

CatOsterman.com. "Biography." http://www.catosterman.com/bio.html.

Cerrone, Matthew. "Stats: David Wright Is a Streaky Hitter." Matthew Cerrone's Mets Blog, June 1, 2009. http://www.metsblog.com/2009/06/01/stats-david -wright-is-a-streaky-hitter/.

Chance, Don M. "What Are the Odds? Another Look at DiMaggio's Streak." *Chance* 22, no. 2 (2009): 33–42.

Chen, Hogan, and James G. Robinson. "Flashback: Young's Losing Streak Snapped at 27. July 28, 1993." BaseballLibrary.com (2006). http://www.baseballlibrary.com /baseballlibrary/features/flashbacks/07_28_1993.stm.

Christianson, Kiel. "University of Chicago Professor Studies Why Some Golfers Choke Under Pressure." *Golf Illinois/Golf Publisher Syndications*, January 30, 2006. http://hpl.uchicago.edu/Popular%20Press/Pop%20PDFs/Golf%20Illinois %202006.pdf.

Clark, Russell D. III. "An Analysis of Players' Consistency Among Professional
Golfers: A Longitudinal Study." *Perceptual and Motor Skills* 101 (2005): 365–72.

———. "An Examination of the 'Hot Hand' in Professional Golfers." *Perceptual
and Motor Skills* 101 (2005): 935–42.

Conyers, Matthew. "Trinity Captures 12th Straight Squash Title." *Hartford
Courant*, February 21, 2010. http://articles.courant.com/2010-02-21/sports
/hc-web-trinity-squash-0222feb22_1_baset-chaudhry-squash-title-trinity.

Costandi, Mo. "Kicking Performance Affects Perception of Goal Size." Science
Blogs, October 12, 2009. http://scienceblogs.com/neurophilosophy/2009
/10/kicking_performance_affects_perception_of_goal_size.php.

Cotton, Christopher, and Joseph Price. "The Hot Hand, Competitive Experience, and
Performance Differences by Gender." Cornell University, Department of Economics
(2006). http://www.people.cornell.edu/pages/csc35/papers/hothand.pdf.

Crasnick, Jerry. "Baseball's Law of Averages." *World Series '07 Official Program*.
(2007): 187–93.

Currie, Bennie M. "Ball from Cubs' Playoff Loss Auctioned for $106,600." *USA
Today*, December 19, 2003. http://www.usatoday.com/sports/baseball/nl/cubs
/2003-12-19-bartman-auction_x.htm.

D3Hoops. "Lincoln Pours in 201 Points," December 2, 2006.
http://www.d3hoops.com/news.php?date=2006-12-02.

D'Aniello, Joe. "DiMaggio's Hitting Streak: High 'Hit Average' the Key." *Baseball
Research Journal* 32 (2003): 31–34.

DaytonFlyers.com. "Johnson's Free Throws Help UD to a 60-59 Overtime Win
Over Auburn," November 28, 2008. http://www.daytonflyers.com/sports
/m-baskbl/recaps/112808aaa.html.

Deadspin.com. "The Pop-Psychologizing of Alex Rodriguez Will Never End",
November 5, 2009. http://deadspin.com/5398226/the-pop+psychologizing
-of-alex-rodriguez-will-never-end.

Deane, Bill. "Gibson Was Great in '68." Baseball Analysts, June 10, 2005.
http://baseballanalysts.com/archives/2005/06/gibson_was_grea_1.php.

Diaconis, Persi, and Frederick Mosteller. "Methods for Studying Coincidences."
Journal of the American Statistical Association 84 (1989): 853–61.

Dorsey-Palmateer, Reid, and Gary Smith. "Bowlers' Hot Hands." *American Statistician* 58 (2004): 38–45.

Douchant, Mike. "Greatest 63 Games in NCAA Tournament History." *USA Today*, March 25, 2002. http://www.usatoday.com/sports/college/basketball/men/02tourney/greatest-games.htm.

Elias Sports Bureau. "Elias Says . . ." ESPN.com, August 15, 2006. http://sports.espn.go.com/espn/news/story?id=2549824.

ESPN.com. "Bucknell Bison Schedule - 2003-04." http://sports.espn.go.com/ncb/teams/schedule?teamId=2083&year=2004.

———. Hurricanes-Bruins play-by-play sheet. http://sports.espn.go.com/nhl/playbyplay?gameId=300410001&period=0.

———. "NHL Statistics Glossary." http://sports.espn.go.com/espn/print?id=2183890&type=story.

———. Raptors-Lakers play-by-play sheet. http://sports.espn.go.com/nba/playbyplay?gameId=260122013.

———. "Saint Louis Billikens Schedule - 2005-06." http://sports.espn.go.com/ncb/teams/schedule?teamId=139&year=2006.

———. Super Bowl XLII (New England Patriots vs. New York Giants) play-by-play sheet. http://espn.go.com/nfl/playbyplay?gameId=280203017&period=0.

ESPN Sports Century. "April Classic Moments: April 1, College Basketball." ESPN.com (not dated). http://espn.go.com/sportscentury/moments/9904.html.

Farkas, Gabe. "Comparing Win/Loss Streaks to Statistical Expectations." *Courtside Times* (original source) / *Internet Archive* (only remaining location), January 24, 2006. http://web.archive.org/web/20070112150812/http://www.courtsidetimes.net/articles/355.

Feller, William. *An Introduction to Probability Theory and Its Applications* vol. 2, 2nd ed. New York: John Wiley, 1971.

Ferraro, Michael X., and John Veneziano. *Numbelievable!: The Dramatic Stories Behind the Most Memorable Numbers in Sports History.* Chicago: Triumph Books, 2007.

FIUsports.com. Baseball season statistics, June 5, 2010. http://www.fiusports.com/fls/11700/Stats_Cumulative/Bball/2010/teamcume.htm.

Fischer, Claude S., Michael Hout, Martin Sanchez Jankowski, Samuel R. Lucas, Ann Swidler, and Kim Voss. *Inequality by Design: Cracking the Bell Curve Myth.* Princeton, NJ: Princeton University Press, 1996.

Fleder, Rob (ed.). *The College Football Book.* New York: Sports Illustrated Books, 2008.

Frey, Jennifer. "For Young, Three Hits and One More Loss." *New York Times* (July 8, 1993). http://www.nytimes.com/1993/07/08/sports/baseball-for-young-three -hits-and-one-more-loss.html?scp=24&sq=%22anthony%20young%22&st=cse.

Gamecock Athletics. "Carolina Opens Super Regional with 15-6 Win Over Georgia: Gamecocks Finish with Eight Home Runs on the Afternoon" (June 10, 2006). http://gamecocksonline.cstv.com/sports/m-basebl/recaps/061006aab.html.

Garber, Greg. "Trinity Squash Takes Unprecedented Streak Further with 11th Straight Title." *ESPN.com* (February 23, 2009). http://sports.espn.go.com/ncaa /news/story?id=3927303.

Gilbert, Daniel T. *Stumbling on Happiness.* New York: Knopf, 2006.

Gilden, David L., and Stephanie Gray Wilson. "Streaks in Skilled Performance." *Psychonomic Bulletin and Review* 2 (1995): 260–65.

Gilovich, Thomas, Robert Vallone, and Amos Tversky. "The Hot Hand in Basketball: On the Misperception of Random Sequences." *Cognitive Psychology* 17 (1985): 295–d314.

Golenbock, Peter. *Wrigleyville: A Magical History Tour of the Chicago Cubs* (updated version). New York: St. Martin's Press, 1999.

Gonzales, Patrick. "'Regular Guy' Beats Odds with Pair of Holes-in-One at Rawls." *Lubbock Avalanche-Journal* (July 31, 2006). http://www.lubbockonline.com /stories/073106/gen_073106020.shtml.

Gould, Stephen Jay. "The Streak of Streaks." *New York Review of Books* 35 (August 18, 1988). http://www.nybooks.com/articles/4337.

Hartwig, Mark. "A Tool That Counts: Basic Statistics for the Amateur Scientist, Part 3. Reasonable Expectations and Helpful Principles." *Citizen Scientist* (April 8, 2005). http://www.sas.org/tcs/weeklyIssues_2005/2005-04-08/feature1 /index.html.

Hein, David. "UCLA's 88-Game Winning Streak: Two Undefeated NCAA Crowns During Nearly Three Perfect Years." *Suite101* (January 5, 2009). http://college -basketball.suite101.com/article.cfm/uclas_88game_winning_streak.

Henderson, David R., and Charles L. Hooper. "When Lady Luck Plays Moneyball." *TCS Daily*, October 20, 2006. http://www.tcsdaily.com/article.aspx?id=102006A.

HockeyGoalies.org, Brian Boucher page. http://hockeygoalies.org/bio/boucher.html.

Hollinger, John. "Ranking the Greatest Finals Performances: No. 10 [Michael Jordan, Chicago, 1992]." ESPN.com, June 12, 2008. http://sports.espn.go.com/nba/playoffs2008/columns/story?columnist=hollinger_john&page=FinalsPerformances-10.

Huizinga, John, and Sandy Weil. "Hot Hand or Hot Head? Overconfidence in Shot Making Ability in the NBA (MIT Sloan Sports Analytics Conference)." Sportsmetricians Consulting, March 7, 2009. http://sportsmetricians.com/.

Hurvich, Clifford. "Winning and Losing Streaks" (class handout, not dated). http://pages.stern.nyu.edu/~churvich/Undergrad/Handouts4/13-Streak.pdf.

International Basketball Federation/Fédération Internationale de Basketball. Kobe Bryant player statistics, 2008 Olympics. http://www.fiba.com/pages/eng/fe/08/olym/men/teamPlay/play/p/competitioncode//eventid/4004/langid/1/langlc/en/playernumber/46997/roundid/4004/season//teamnumber/379/fe_teamPlay_playStat.html.

James, Bill. "Evidence of Non-Random Clusters in the Career Performance of George Brett and Tony Gwynn." *Hot Hand in Sports* (July 28, 2005; old version of website, which is no longer online. This paper is available upon request from Alan Reifman, alan.reifman@ttu.edu).

———. "Underestimating the Fog." *Baseball Research Journal* 33 (2004): 29–33. http://www.sabr.org/cmsfiles/underestimating.pdf.

Kanter, Rosabeth Moss. *Confidence: How Winning Streaks and Losing Streaks Begin and End.* New York: Crown Business, 2004.

Kelley, Brent. "Byron Nelson's 1945 Tournament Results." About.com (not dated). http://golf.about.com/od/golfersmen/a/nelson_1945_pga.htm.

———. "Most Consecutive Wins on the PGA Tour." About.com (not dated). http://golf.about.com/od/progolftours/qt/pgaconswins.htm.

Keri, Jonah. "Forty Years Later, Gibson's 1.12 ERA Remains Magic Number." ESPN.com, February 7, 2008. http://sports.espn.go.com/espn/blackhistory2008/columns/story?page=keri/080221.

King, Bruce M., and Edward M. Minium. *Statistical Reasoning in the Behavioral Sciences* 5th ed. Hoboken, NJ: Wiley, 2008.

Klaassen, Franc J. G. M., and Jan R. Magnus. "Are Points in Tennis Independent and Identically Distributed? Evidence from a Dynamic Binary Panel Data Model." *Journal of the American Statistical Association* 96 (2001): 500–9.

Koehler, Jonathan Jay, and Caryn A. Conley. "The Hot Hand Myth in Professional Basketball." *Journal of Sport and Exercise Psychology* 25 (2003): 253–59.

Lackritz, James R. "Two of Baseball's Great Marks: Can They Ever be Broken?" *Chance* 9 (1996): 12–18.

LakerStats.com. "Great Moments in Laker History: Kobe Bryant Creates NBA Records," January 7, 2003. http://www.lakerstats.com/moment.php?articleid=010703.

Levitt, Steven, and Stephen Dubner. *Freakonomics: A Rogue Economist Explores the Hidden Side of Everything*. New York: Morrow, 2005.

Lewis, Michael. *Moneyball: The Art of Winning an Unfair Game*. New York: Norton, 2003.

Livingston, Jeffrey A. "The Hot Hand and the Cold Hand in Professional Golf." Bentley University, Department of Economics (2007). http://papers.ssrn.com/sol3/papers.cfm?abstract_id=1157159.

Lyman, Shelby. "On Chess: Slumps Uncommon in Royal Game." *Columbus Dispatch*, June 27, 2009. http://www.dispatch.com/live/content/life/stories /2009/06/27/2_chess0627.ART_ART_06-27-09_D2_49E82KR.html?type =rss&cat=&sid=101.

Manuel, John. "Making Sense of Fresno: Six Ways to Comprehend the Bulldogs' Amazing Title Run." Baseball America, June 25, 2008. http://www.baseballamerica.com/today/college/column/2008/266393.html

McCotter, Trent. "DiMaggio's Challengers." *Baseball Research Journal* 35 (2006): 82–83.

———. "Hitting Streaks Don't Obey Your Rules: Evidence that Hitting Streaks Aren't Just By-Products of Random Variation." *Baseball Research Journal* 37 (2008): 62–70.

———. "More on Streaks." *Baseball Research Journal* 36 (2007): 44–45.

MLB.com. "Four Straight Homers in One Game." *History of the Game* (updated August 11, 2010). http://mlb.mlb.com/mlb/history/rare_feats/index.jsp ?feature=four_straight_homers.

Moran, Malcolm. "Leinart Carries Southern Cal to Dramatic Defeat of Notre Dame." USA Today, October 16, 2005. http://www.usatoday.com/sports /college/football/games/2005-10-15-usc-notre-dame_x.htm.

Myers, David G. *Intuition: Its Powers and Perils.* New Haven, CT: Yale University Press, 2002.

NBA.com. Derek Fisher career statistics. http://www.nba.com/playerfile/derek_fisher /career_stats.html.

NCAA. 2008–2009 men's basketball records (Division I). http://fs.ncaa.org/Docs/stats/m_basketball_RB/2009/D1.pdf.

New York Times. "NCAA Tournament: Women; Texas Tech, down by 17-0, shocks Irish," March 26, 2000. http://www.nytimes.com/2000/03/26/sports/ncaa -tournament-women-texas-tech-down-by-17-0-shocks-irish.html.

Neyer, Rob. "Figuring Out the A's Winning Streak." ESPN.com, February 10, 2003. http://sports.espn.go.com/mlb/columns/story?columnist=neyer_rob&id=1506830.

———. "Figuring Out the Laws of Probability." ESPN.com, February 5, 2003. http://sports.espn.go.com/mlb/columns/story?columnist=neyer_rob&id =1504386.

Orenstein, David. "On the Golf Tee or the Pitcher's Mound, Brain Dooms Motion to Inconsistency. Study: Movement Not Primarily a Mechanical Phenomenon." Stanford Report, January 17, 2007. http://news-service.stanford.edu/news /2007/january17/movement-011707.html.

Oskarsson, An T., Leaf Van Boven, Gary H. McClelland, and Reid Hastie. "What's Next? Judging Sequences of Binary Events." *Psychological Bulletin* 135 (2009): 262–85.

Paulos, John Allen. "Does Joe DiMaggio's Streak Deserve an Asterisk? Report Suggests Slugger May Have Gained from Yankees' Relationship with Official Scorer." ABC News, October 7, 2007. http://abcnews.go.com/Technology /WhosCounting/story?id=3694104&page=1.

Peters, Ken. "Giguere, Mighty Ducks Get Clean Sweep of the Wild." USA Today, May 17, 2003. http://www.usatoday.com/sports/hockey/cup/2003-05-17-ducks -wild-game-4_x.htm.

Pomeroy, Ken. "Bucking the Trend." KenPom.com Blog, December 3, 2003. http://kenpom.com/blog/index.php/weblog/bucking_the_trend.

———. "Move the Line Back." KenPom.com Blog, January 19, 2005. http://kenpom.com/blog/index.php/weblog/move_the_line_back.

Posner, Richard A. *A Failure of Capitalism: The Crisis of '08 and the Descent into Depression.* Cambridge, MA: Harvard University Press, 2009.

Pro Football Hall of Fame. "Miami's Perfect Season" (not dated). http://www.profootballhof.com/history/decades/1970s/miami.aspx.

Reifman, Alan. Analysis of NHL hardest shot contest. Hot Hand in Sports Blog, January 25, 2007. http://thehothand.blogspot.com/2007/01/for-athlete-to -exhibit-hot-hand-say-by.html.

———. "Hot Hand? Kobe Bryant's 81-point game." 82 Games, 2007. http://www.82games.com/kobe81.htm.

Rockoff, David M., and Phil A. Yates. "Chasing DiMaggio: Streaks in Simulated Seasons Using Non-Constant At-Bats." *Journal of Quantitative Analysis in Sports* 5, no. 2 (2009): http://www.bepress.com/jqas/vol5/iss2/4.

Rosen, Charley. *The Pivotal Season.* New York: Thomas Dunne, 2005.

Ross, Lee, David Greene, and Pamela House. "The False Consensus Effect: An Egocentric Bias in Social Perception and Attribution Processes." *Journal of Experimental Social Psychology* 13 (1977): 279–301.

Santoliquito, Joseph. "Lincoln Sets D-III Record for Points in Game, Half." ESPN.com, December 3, 2006. http://sports.espn.go.com/ncb/news/story?id =2683783.

Sela, Rebecca J., and Jeffrey S. Simonoff. "Does Momentum Exist in a Baseball Game?" In *Statistical Thinking in Sports,* edited by Jim Albert and Ruud H. Koning, 135–51. Boca Raton, FL: Chapman & Hall/CRC, 2007.

Sexton, Joe. "Don't Pin This Loss on Young." *New York Times,* June 2, 1993. http://www.nytimes.com/1993/06/02/sports/baseball-don-t-pin-this-loss-on -young.html?scp=16&sq=%22anthony+young%22+mets&st=nyt.

Shouler, Ken. "Zoning In: It's Called The Zone—An Elevated State of Consciousness and Focus Where Athletes Perform Beyond Normal Levels. But Is It Real?" *Cigar Aficionado* (December 2007): 186–95. Also available online, http://www.winespectator.com/Cigar/CA_Archives/CA_Show_Article /0,2322,2085,00.html.

Simmons, Bill. *The Book of Basketball: The NBA According to the Sports Guy.* New York: ESPN Books, 2009.

Singer, Tom. "For Derby, Hamilton Calls on Old Friend: Rangers Outfielder Will Have Former Mentor Throw to Him." *MLB.com* (July 14, 2008). http://mlb.mlb.com /news/article.jsp?ymd=20080714&content_id=3135534&vkey=allstar2008 &fext=.jsp.

———. "Phillies' Comeback a Part of Sport's Lore: Baseball Has Long History of Teams Making Up Huge Deficits." MLB.com, September 30, 2007. http://mlb.mlb.com/news/article.jsp?ymd=20070930&content_id=2243096.

Smith, Gary. "Horseshoe Pitchers' Hot Hands." *Psychonomic Bulletin & Review* 10 (2003): 753–58.

Spencer, Dan. Broadcast, Fox 34 News, Lubbock, Texas, May 18, 2009.

Sports Illustrated on Campus. "Hot or Not: The Sizzlers and Fizzlers from the Week that Was" (February 6, 2006). http://sportsillustrated.cnn.com/2006 /sioncampus/02/06/hot.not4/index.html.

Sports Illustrated (SI) Vault. "The Micheal Williams Streak" (April 13, 1998). http://vault.sportsillustrated.cnn.com/vault/article/magazine/MAG1012556 /index.htm.

Stadler, Mike. *The Psychology of Baseball: Inside the Mental Game of the Major League Player.* New York: Gotham, 2007.

Steiner, Ivan D. *Group Processes and Productivity.* New York: Academic Press, 1972.

Stephens, Bailey. "Wittels Two Shy of NCAA Hit Streak Mark: With FIU Eliminated, Slugger Must Wait Until Next Season." MLB.com, June 5, 2010. http://mlb.mlb.com/news/article.jsp?ymd=20100605&content_id=10826670.

St. John, Allen. *Made to Be Broken: The 50 Greatest Records and Streaks in Sports.* Chicago: Triumph Books, 2006.

Strogatz, Steven. *Sync: The Emerging Science of Spontaneous Order.* New York: Theia, 2003.

Studeman, Dave. "Ten Things About Momentum in the Postseason." Hardball Times, September 29, 2005. http://www.hardballtimes.com/main/article /ten-things-about-momentum-in-the-postseason.

Tango, Tom, Mitchel Lichtman, and Andrew Dolphin. *The Book: Playing the Percentages in Baseball.* Washington, DC: Potomac Books, 2007.

TexasSports.com. University of Texas softball archives. http://www.texassports.com /sports/w-softbl/archive/tex-w-softbl-archive.html.

Timmermann, Tom. "Perfection Is Open to Interpretation: Even an Undefeated Season, as UConn is Seeking Tonight, Is a Longshot That Overcomes Mistakes." *St. Louis Post-Dispatch,* April 7, 2009. http://www.stltoday.com/sports/article _35543faf-267a-5438-8434-ee88cd89a26d.html.

Trinity Athletics. "Trinity Men's Squash Tops Yale in Dramatic Fashion for 13th Straight National Championship Title" (February 27, 2011). http://athletics.trincoll.edu/sports/msquash/2010-11/releases/Men-s _Squash_G_201011.

UCLA Academic Technology Services. "Statistical Computing Seminars: Introduction to Power Analysis" (not dated). http://www.ats.ucla.edu/stat/seminars/Intro_power /default.htm.

Warrack, Giles. "The Great Streak." *Chance* 8 (1995): 41–43, 60.

White, Gordon S. Jr. "Nearly Perfect Is Good Enough." *New York Times,* March 26, 1973. http://www.nytimes.com/packages/html/sports/year_in_sports/03.26b.html.

Wikipedia. "Byron Nelson." http://en.wikipedia.org/wiki/Byron_Nelson.

———. "Housing Bubble." http://en.wikipedia.org/wiki/Housing_bubble.

———. "Joe DiMaggio." http://en.wikipedia.org/wiki/Joe_dimaggio.

———. "Longest NCAA Division I Football Winning Streaks." http://en.wikipedia.org/wiki/Longest_NCAA_Division_I_football_winning_streaks.

———. "MLB Consecutive Games Played Streaks." http://en.wikipedia.org/wiki /MLB_consecutive_games_played_streaks.

———. "NBA Records." http://en.wikipedia.org/wiki/NBA_records.

———. "United States Triple Crown of Thoroughbred Racing." http://en.wikipedia.org/wiki/United_States_Triple_Crown_of_Thoroughbred _Racing.

Wilke, Andreas, and H. Clark Barrett. "The Hot Hand Phenomenon as a Cognitive Adaptation to Clumped Resources." *Evolution and Human Behavior* 30 (2009): 161–69.

Winston, Wayne L. *Mathletics: How Gamblers, Managers, and Sports Enthusiasts Use Mathematics in Baseball, Basketball, and Football.* Princeton, NJ: Princeton University Press, 2009.

Wolff, Alexander. "The Man Couldn't Miss: Christian Laettner's Perfect Shooting Propelled Duke to its Fifth Consecutive Final Four." Sports Illustrated (SI) Vault, April 6, 1992. http://vault.sportsillustrated.cnn.com/vault/article /magazine/MAG1003607/index.htm.

ONLINE RESOURCES

Hot Hand in Sports
   http://thehothand.blogspot.com

Inside the Book: Streaks Page
   http://www.insidethebook.com/ee/index.php/weblog/C31/

Numbers Guy (*Wall Street Journal*)
   http://blogs.wsj.com/numbersguy/

Research Randomizer (online random-number generator for anyone wishing to carry out simulation analyses of sports performances)
   http://www.randomizer.org/

Retrosheet (box scores for virtually any game in Major League Baseball history)
   http://www.retrosheet.org/

INDEX

ABOUT THE AUTHOR

Alan Reifman, PhD, is Professor of Human Development and Family Studies at Texas Tech University. In addition to conducting research on the transition from adolescence to adulthood and the development of heavy drinking during this time, Reifman regularly teaches graduate statistics courses in his department. Since 2002, Reifman has combined his interests in sports streaks and statistical analysis to operate the Hot Hand in Sports website, the outgrowth of which is this book.